Reprints of Economic Classics

THE PAPER POUND OF 1797-1821

THE

PAPER POUND

OF

1797-1821

THE BULLION REPORT

8TH JUNE 1810

EDITED WITH AN INTRODUCTION BY

EDWIN CANNAN

SECOND EDITION

[1925]

REPRINTS OF ECONOMIC CLASSICS

AUGUSTUS M. KELLEY · PUBLISHERS
NEW YORK 1969

This Edition First Published 1919

Second Edition 1925

(London: P. S. King & Son Ltd., *Orchard House,*
Westminster, 1925)

Reprinted 1969 by

AUGUSTUS M. KELLEY · PUBLISHERS

New York   New York   10010

By Arrangement with Frank Cass & Co Ltd, *London*

SBN 678 00536 2

L C N 67-24748

THE PAPER POUND
OF 1797–1821

First Published . . . 1919
Second Edition . . . 1925

THE PAPER POUND
of 1797–1821

A REPRINT OF
THE BULLION REPORT

WITH AN INTRODUCTION BY

EDWIN CANNAN, M.A., LL.D.
Professor of Political Economy in the University of London

SECOND EDITION

LONDON
P. S. KING & SON, LTD.
ORCHARD HOUSE, WESTMINSTER
—
1925

PREFACE TO THE SECOND EDITION

In 1914 no economic truth had been longer or more generally recognised than that limitation of amount is essential to the preservation of the value of any article or service. It was universally admitted that things available in unlimited quantities had no value, and when anything became more plentiful, everyone expected it to become less valuable, in the absence, of course, of counteracting circumstances on the side of demand. Few persons, it is true, could explain clearly why plenty and cheapness should thus go together, even after the theory of marginal utility had made its great contribution towards a satisfactory solution of the question, but the fact was so amply established by experience that no one disbelieved it as a general rule. Here and there somebody would be found to deny that this "quantity theory," which admittedly applied to everything else, was applicable to currency, but none of them had ever been able to explain why currency should be an exception, while there was ample experience to show that it was not. Disastrous experiments with insufficiently limited issues of paper currency like the assignats gave warning against the abandonment of due limitation, and successful experiments in the maintenance of silver and base-metal coinages at a par with gold had shown conclusively that proper control of the amount of a currency could in fact regulate its value or purchasing power. The effect of the discovery and development of the Australian and South African gold-fields upon the purchasing power of currencies which (owing to free coinage and freedom to export or melt down coin) were interchangeable with gold bullion, was well known, and gave rise to much discussion of plans for dissociating the control of the amount, and consequently the purchasing power of currency, from the chances of gold discoveries.

But while there was a general appreciation of the fact that currency is no exception to the general law of value that plenty and cheapness go together, there was a widespread, almost universal, popular absence of understanding of the manner in which the value of convertible paper currency is regulated. When such a currency is convertible on demand into gold which the holder may freely use for any purpose or export, the whole currency, whether a large or small proportion of it consists of paper, cannot except for a moment be appreciably in excess of the amount which can circulate at par with gold bullion. If the whole currency exceeds this amount, its purchasing power over gold bullion must fall, and it becomes profitable to melt down or export gold coin or gold bars if these bars can be obtained at the Mint price. In order to get gold coin or bars at that price people begin to present paper currency for redemption : the paper so redeemed is cancelled, while the coin or bars issued to redeem it do not take its place, because they are melted or exported. The whole currency is reduced in amount until its value is restored to par with gold bullion. Convertibility thus keeps the paper at par with bullion by limiting its amount— limiting it "automatically" no doubt, but still limiting it. But this was very far from being generally understood. People saw that to make sure that they could meet any demand for redemption, the issuers of convertible paper currency kept "reserves" of gold, and they imagined that these reserves in some mysterious way directly supported the value of the paper. They would even call the reserves " backing " for the notes, or say the reserves were " behind " the notes.

This was the error in popular ideas about money which led to the great currency disasters of the years following 1914. What motives inspired nearly every government in the world to suspend convertibility, and whether those motives were good or bad is of very little importance. What was vitally important and did all the mischief was the general failure to recognise that when convertibility into free bullion is absent, some other system of limitation must be present unless the currency is to be indefinitely increased and its value indefinitely diminished. Far from inventing any new system of limitation to take the place of convertibility, governments took steps to remove or render inoperative any legal obstructions to the increase of currency which happened to have been in force alongside of convertibility. In the United Kingdom, for example, the provision that no banknotes could be issued above a certain low limit except against an equal amount of gold held by the issuing banks was rendered nugatory by the creation of a Currency Note issue subject to no such restriction. In some other countries existing limitations of issue to definite fixed sums were removed.

The consequences, so far as they had appeared in October 1919, are briefly indicated on pp. xxxix and xl of the Introduction. It had been suggested to the publishers that the situation was so similar to that in which this country found itself in 1810 that it would be well to reprint the Bullion Report of that year, in which the question had been well thrashed out. They adopted the suggestion and asked me to write an Introduction. I have been blamed for making this so exclusively historical in character, but that was inevitable, as I had dealt with the general theory of the subject in another work, *Money, its connexion with rising and falling prices*, of which the first edition was published in 1918. I might also plead that many of the critics seem to have found much more theory than they liked.

Nothing in the book excited more attention and hostile comment than the suggestion on p. xli of the Introduction that when the scales fell from the eyes of the people of Europe they would demand that their governments should burn enough paper money to restore their currencies to par with gold. Taking this literally as a prophecy I admit some disappointment. The nations have shown themselves on the whole stupider than I expected, and the scales stuck on their eyes so long that simple restoration by reduction became impossible in many cases. In the others, including that of Great Britain, Australia and South Africa, the process of restoration has been far too prolonged, with many unpleasant results, among others the fact that it is not now only the dollar which the pound cannot " look in the face," but the German mark and several other European currencies which are at this moment at par with gold and will remain there unless their managers once more forget the doctrine of due limitation of supply. But taking the suggestion of burning paper money as advice rather than prophecy no one can say that it has not been amply justified by subsequent history. The countries which limited and reduced their currencies have won through with far less damage than those which failed to do so.

Readers will do well to remember that when the Introduction was written and passed for press, the British Treasury had not yet made its great resolve to stop the indefinite increase of the Currency Note issue by adopting the Cunliffe limitation. The announcement of that resolve was made in December, 1919, and coincided so nearly with the publication of this book that the Treasury Minute and a presentation copy of the *Paper Pound* very appropriately arrived at the Bank of England on the same day. In October, 1919, there was nothing to show that the

British government would not allow the pound sterling to continue its course on the slippery slope down which the German mark subsequently slid to the one-billionth level.

The alterations which I have made in the present edition of the Introduction are not too numerous to specify for the satisfaction of possessors of the first. On p. vii I have introduced a mention of the number of grains of pure gold contained in a sovereign because it appears that the inexpert are often confused by the fact that in our day an ounce of gold is usually understood to be an ounce of pure gold, the Mint price of which is approximately 84s. 11½d., whereas in the time of the Bullion Report an ounce of gold was in England taken to be an ounce of " standard gold," of which only 22 carats out of 24, or eleven-twelfths, is pure gold, the rest being alloy ; in the Introduction it would have been very inconvenient to depart from the practice followed in the Bullion Report itself, so that the reader must understand prices of gold to be prices of " standard " gold. On p. viii I have rewritten the paragraph about the position of the silver coin, as it was not absolutely correct.   On p. xiv I have made a small change to avoid implying that the melting down of gold coin was prohibited from the beginning of the war of 1914–18. And on p. xxxiv line 9, I have substituted " the end was hastened " for the slightly inaccurate " all was set aside."   I thank the various critics who have pointed out the need of these corrections.

In the Report itself the lynx eye of Mr. Hawtrey noticed, in the *Economic Journal* for March, 1920, that " 3 dwts." in the middle of p. 31 should be " 13 dwts."   The error, as he notes, occurs in the original folio edition and is copied by the octavo edition of 1810, which the 1919 reprint follows, but as the figure is given correctly in the Minutes of Evidence, I have altered it.   More disconcerting was the discovery of " few " for " new " which Professor Foxwell kindly communicated to me. This led me to collate the 1919 reprint with the original folio edition with the following results, which may as well be recorded, though none of them are of any great importance :—

In addition to correcting, with " parade," as Mr. Hawtrey complains, " security " into " scarcity " on p. 47, the octavo edition of 1810 made in silence four equally sound corrections of the folio text by altering " pass " into " passes " on p. 10 line 21, " and " into " he " on p. 33 line 33, " are " into " is " on p. 46 line 14, and " derived " into " devised " on p. 65 line 25. On the other hand, in the excitement of altering " security " it quite wrongly put " measures " instead of " measure " on p. 47 line 20, and it also omitted the blank space on p. 66 which separates the arguments of the Committee from their conclusions. These two mistakes, which were reproduced in the 1919 edition, are now rectified, as well as the few others which that edition can claim as its own, namely, p. 3 line 2, " Gold Bullion " in small letters instead of capitals, p. 19 line 18, " definite " for " definitive," p. 33 line 25, " discount " for " discounts," p. 39 line 11, " few " for " new," p. 40 line 8, " with " for " which," and lines 32 and 33 brackets omitted, p. 48 line 17, bracket omitted, p. 55, " £ " omitted at top of three columns of the table, p. 57 line 25, " porportion " for " proportion," p. 58 line 8, " modes " for " mode," p. 63 line 10, " year " for " years," p. 67 line 24, " That " for " The," p. 68 line 7, " breath " for " breach," and p. 69 line 25, " definitely " for " definitively."

EDWIN CANNAN.

LONDON SCHOOL OF ECONOMICS,
   Nov. 20, 1924.

CONTENTS

INTRODUCTION

§ 1. War—Crisis—Suspension of Payment

When war broke out with France in February, 1793, the pound sterling, which with its subdivisions, the shilling and the penny, formed the "£ s. d." in which all English money accounts and contracts were expressed, was (as it was again from 1821 to 1914) interchangeable with 123¼ grains of 22 carat ("standard") gold, which equals 113 grains of fine gold. Owing to variations in the rating of the gold and silver coins which took place long before, there was indeed no gold coin representing £1, but the gold coins called guineas (because the gold from which the first issue of them was made came from the Guinea Coast) passed for twenty-one twentieths of £1, half-guineas for twenty-one fortieths, and seven-shilling pieces for seven twentieths, and these gold coins were all legal tender to any amount at those rates. One troy pound of 22 carat gold was coined into 44½ guineas, and anyone who had gold could demand that the Mint should coin it for him at that rate, but in practice he found it better to accept the slightly lower price, £46 10s. the pound or £3 17s. 6d. the ounce, given on the spot by the Bullion Office of the Bank of England. Gold was thus freely "convertible" into coin, and though the law forbade exportation of coin and of bullion produced by melting it, this seems in practice to have had so small an effect that the coin was in fact readily convertible into gold for mintage in foreign countries and for industrial uses both at home and abroad, whenever any appreciable profit presented itself.

Nominally silver was as freely convertible into coin as gold. But in fact, as the Mint price of silver was below the market price, no additions to the silver coin were made. On the other hand the coins in circulation were so much abraded that it was not profitable to melt them down to secure the market price of silver bullion. The silver coinage had thus become a subsidiary coinage maintained at its nominal value by limitation of supply.

There was no legal-tender paper. Bank of England notes, promising to pay the bearer on demand £10, £20, and a few larger sums, circulated freely in London and the immediate neighbourhood. Outside that area there were in circulation similar notes for sums of £5 and upwards, issued by over two hundred banks with less than six partners, called the " country banks " because the London private banks had long ago abandoned the business of issuing notes. The country banks did not go below £5, because the law had forbidden smaller notes since 1777 ; the Bank of England's abstention from issuing £5 notes (maintained by it till soon after the beginning of the war) seems to have been due to mere conservatism—it had only begun to issue £10 notes in 1759. The whole amount of Bank of England notes in circulation was about 12 millions : the amount of country notes is unknown, but later statistics suggest that it may have been not far off the same figure. The amount of gold coin in the country is supposed to have been from 20 to 30 millions, but it must be remembered that a far larger proportion than in modern times would be locked away in hoards only coming into circulation at long intervals.

The business of banking was still very imperfectly understood. Failures of country banks were frequent, and the Bank of England often had moments of anxiety caused by these failures and by its own inability to resist the prevalent feeling of the public by being cautious in lending in times of speculation and liberal during depressions and alarms. It was apt to change its policy too late, so that it continued liberal advances when drawing in was required, and began to draw in when it was no longer desirable to do so, with the natural result of disaster accompanied by confusing recriminations about the comparative advantages of the " restrictive " and the ' expansive " policies, both of which were right if only adopted at the proper time. Moreover, the legal prohibition of all interest above 5 per cent often stood in the way of effective restriction.

The near approach of the war in the winter of 1792–3 caused or coincided with considerable trouble among the country banks, which spread to London, and was only prevented from causing complete disaster by the Government undertaking to lend five millions of Exchequer bills to merchants in difficulties. This offer restored confidence, and bills for only £2,200,000 were actually issued.

Nearly two years of the war passed away without much financial difficulty, but towards the end of 1794 the Bank directors began to complain of Pitt's excessive demands for accommodation. The public expenditure had at first risen but slowly, as may be seen in Table I. on p. xliii. below. Including the expenditure of Ireland, it had been under $17\frac{1}{2}$ millions in 1792, and it was only $24\frac{1}{4}$ millions in 1793 and $29\frac{1}{2}$ in 1794. But the revenue had scarcely increased at all ; it was $19\frac{1}{4}$ millions in 1792 and only $20\frac{1}{4}$ in 1794. In a country with an aggregate income of between 200 and 300 millions mostly belonging to a poor population, even the nine millions borrowed in some way or other by the Government in 1794 must have been a large sum in proportion to the usual annual savings of the people. In 1795 and 1796, however, the public expenditure shot up to

51¾ and 57¾ millions, while the revenue was only 20 and 21½ millions. It is utterly impossible to believe either that the aggregate produce of the nation's labour had risen so that this enormous increase of government expenditure could be met without any reduction of individual consumption and investment, or that the consumption and investment by individuals had been cut down as much as the Government expenditure rose, and it is wholly improbable that increase of production and reduction of private consumption and investment would together anything like counterbalance the increase of Government expenditure. Doubtless what has constantly happened in great wars was happening in this country in 1795-6: the Government and people together were spending much more money than they could go on spending without either a sharp monetary crisis leading to a reduction of the aggregate money expenditure or a dilution of the currency which enables the large money expenditure to go on by providing a larger nominal amount of money to be expended in the purchase of the same amount of goods and services—at higher prices. In a country of compromise it was to be expected that both of these alternatives would be embraced.

At the end of February, 1794, as is shown in Table II. on p. xliv. below, the Bank of England held almost 7 millions of coin and bullion while its liabilities were less than 18¾ millions (of which 10¼ were notes in circulation). Next year the position was only a little less favourable, but in 1796 the coin and bullion had shrunk to 2½ millions while the liabilities had only gone down to 16½ millions. On August 31 the coin and bullion had gone down another £400,000, while the liabilities were still almost 16 millions. By what particular incidents the crisis was finally precipitated is of little importance. It arrived at the end of February, 1797. The coin and bullion in the Bank was reduced to so small an amount and the drain was continuing at such a rate that the directors informed Pitt that the situation was desperate. In similar circumstances a modern government would declare a bank holiday of three days, and spend the interval in printing and securing authorisation for legal tender government notes, which it would then lend to the Bank to be paid out instead of coin. Pitt adopted a less simple but equally effective plan. First thing on Sunday morning, February 26, he secured the attendance of the King, the Lord Chancellor, the Lord President, the Duke of Portland, Marquis Cornwallis, Earl Spencer, the Earl of Liverpool, Lord Grenville and himself at a Council which passed and communicated at once to the Bank a resolution which declared "the unanimous opinion of the Board that it is indispensably necessary for the public service that the Directors of the Bank of England should forbear issuing any cash in payment until the sense of Parliament can be taken on that subject and the proper measures adopted thereupon for maintaining the means of circulation and supporting the public and commercial credit of the kingdom at this important conjuncture," and "required" the directors "on the grounds of the exigency of the case to conform thereto until the sense of Parliament can be taken as aforesaid."

Opening as usual on Monday morning, the Bank prudently made no attempt to explain why the order was issued, but exhibited it along with the following notice :

"The Governor, Deputy-Governor, and Directors of the Bank of England think it their duty to inform the proprietors of Bank Stock as well as the Public at large that the general concerns of the Bank are in the most affluent and prosperous situation, and such as to preclude every doubt as to the security of its notes. The Directors mean to continue their usual discounts for the accommodation of the commercial interest, paying the amount in bank-notes, and the dividend warrants will be paid in the same manner."

At noon a great meeting of merchants and bankers was held which passed a resolution undertaking to accept bank-notes, and eventually 4,000 signatures were attached to this.

On the same day the King thought it " proper to communicate to the House of Commons without delay the measure adopted to obviate the effects which might be occasioned by the unusual demand of specie lately made from different parts of the country on the metropolis." His Majesty did not apparently think it proper to refer in any way to the difficulties caused by his Minister's demands on the Bank, nor did Pitt himself when he proceeded to present the Minute of Council recording Sunday's resolution and to move for a committee to inquire into the outstanding engagements of the Bank. He said he would propose that the liabilities of the Bank should be secured by the State (an intention never carried out), and that its notes should be accepted in all payments due to it. In answer to questions he declined to say whether he favoured making the notes legal tender or not, and said he would bring in a Bill to allow the issue (by all banks) of notes for sums less than £5. Fox and other speakers expressed the utmost consternation, and prophesied that the notes would go the way of assignats. Next day in the House of Lords the Government announced that they had decided against making the notes legal tender. Lansdowne gloomily asseverated, "A fever is as much a fever in London as in Paris or Amsterdam . . . . the fall will be slow perhaps, and gradual for a time ; but it will be certain."

The Order in Council was confirmed by the Act 37 Geo. III. c. 45, called the "Bank Restriction Act," passed on May 3. How temporary the emergency was supposed to be is shown by the fact that this act was only to continue till June 24 : in fact it was kept in force by continuing acts for nearly quarter of a century.

An Act (37 Geo. III. c. 32) had been passed three days earlier to suspend the prohibition embodied in the Act of 1777 and thus allow the issue of bank-notes for sums under £5 down to but not below £1. Nothing in the legislation made bank notes legal tender, nor was there any provision for country and Scotch banks. From the time when the news of the Order in Council reached them, these banks had apparently acted as if the Restriction required them as well as the Bank of England to refrain from cash payments. But they did not claim to be able to insist on paying out nothing except their own notes, like the Bank of England. They had always been ready to give Bank of England notes or drafts on London in exchange for their own notes, and continued to be so. Consequently though their notes were not convertible into coin, they were always convertible into Bank of England notes, and thus each bank remained subject to the ordinary limitations. It was the Bank of England alone which was relieved from all fear of being asked to give other money for its notes.

Gold coin was soon little seen, much of it being exported and most of the rest put away in hoards. Silver, required for all payments under £1 in the absence of half-guineas and seven-shilling pieces, was very scarce, and the want of national coins was to some extent relieved by the stamping of foreign dollars with the King's head and by the Bank issuing silver tokens for 5s. : why these should have been issued by the Bank as tokens instead of by the Mint as coins does not appear.

The currency situation thus created differed from that which prevailed after August 1914 in several ways. In the earlier period there was no legal tender paper, while in the latter both Treasury notes and Bank of England notes were legal tender to any amount. On the other hand, in the earlier period Bank of England notes were inconvertible, whereas, in the later, Bank of England notes were convertible into Treasury notes and Treasury notes could be converted into gold coin by any one who was not afraid of being called unpatriotic, and, after 1916, of being suspected of an intention of breaking the law which prohibited melting the coin of the realm. But neither of these differences are important. Under the Restriction Act of 1797 the Government was bound to accept and pay Bank of England Notes as equivalent to the pounds sterling which the Bank still promised on the face of the note to pay. The ordinary law-abiding private individual, whatever the comparative value of note and bullion, could gain nothing by refusing notes and insisting on guineas, because he was unable to smuggle them abroad or to melt them down and swear that the bullion was not produced from coin of the realm. Such guineas as remained in circulation or were brought from hoards from time to time could only be passed in respectable circles for a pound and a shilling, and no one seems to have thought of treating a guinea as 21s., and a pound-note as, say, only 19s. The £1 of the note issue became the standard £1 in 1797 just as later in 1914. The convertibility of Treasury notes into sovereigns which continued all through the war of 1914–18 made no real difference, since transport difficulties prevented the exportation of sovereigns and from December 1916 legal prohibition of melting them was in force. When transport difficulties ceased to operate, a prohibition of export was promptly issued. As sovereigns could only be used for currency, for which purpose £1 notes were just as good, there was no inducement to ask for them in place of notes.

It must not be supposed that the transition of 1797 from a metallic to a paper standard was effected with a total absence of disturbance and confusion. *The Memoirs of a Banking House*, by a Scotch banker, Sir William Forbes, published long after the need for professing a confidence which was not felt had passed away, provide a useful supplement to the dry bones of official notices and brief newspaper reports of meetings.   Sir William says that a meeting called by the Lord-Lieutenant of Midlothian to concert measures for the defence of the country in case of invasion and reported in the Edinburgh newspapers of Feb 18 caused a panic among the farmers and lower classes of country people.

" On Monday the 20th," he continues (p. 82), " they came to our counting-house in considerable numbers, evidently under the impression of terror, calling for payment of their notes that had been lodged at interest.   This lasted the whole of that week and the two first days of the following.   Nor was it confined to us alone, for the public banks experienced it in a still greater degree, and we were beginning to think there was to be a similar, perhaps a still severer, demand on us than what had taken place in 1793 ; when, early in the morning of Wednesday, the 1st March, an express arrived from London to the directors of the Bank of Scotland from Thomas Coutts & Co., their correspondents there, informing them that the demand for gold on the Bank of England had risen to such an alarming height that the Directors had thought it proper to state the circumstance to the Chancellor of the Exchequer, who immediately procured an order of the Privy Council to be issued, prohibiting that bank from making any more issues of specie in exchange for their notes.   Mr. Mansfield, who was a director of the Bank of Scotland, informed our Mr. Anderson of this interesting event, and he immediately brought the intelligence to me, a little before the usual hour of commencing business.   My ideas, at various times during the course of the war, had been often not a little gloomy when I thought of the state of things in the kingdom, and indeed in Europe ; but now it was that I certainly did think the nation was ruined beyond redemption, when so novel and alarming a circumstance had taken place at the Bank of England, which had ever been considered as the bulwark of public and private credit.   Mr. Hay, Mr. Anderson, my son and I all repaired as fast as possible to the counting-house, which at ten o'clock was crowded as usual with people demanding gold.   We were soon joined by Mr. Simpson, cashier, and Mr. James, deputy-governor of the Royal Bank, and by Mr. Fraser, the treasurer of the Bank of Scotland, and we sent for Mr. Hog, manager of the British Linen Company, for all ceremony or etiquette of public or private banks was now out of the question, when it had become necessary to think of what was to be done for our joint preservation on such an emergency. Thence we repaired to the Bank of Scotland, where their directors were assembled, and after some time spent in consultation with them. it was agreed that there was no choice left but to follow the Bank of England, and suspend all further payments in specie. The Lord Provost instantly gave orders for calling a meeting of the principal inhabitants that day at two o'clock, which was very numerously attended, considering the shortness of the notice. . . . After stating the order of Council for suspending the payments in specie by the Bank of England, and the similar resolution taken by the banks of Edinburgh, a resolution was instantly and unanimously entered into by those present to give every countenance and support to the Edinburgh banks—including our firm—by receiving their notes in payment with the same readiness as heretofore, and a handbill was instantly circulated over Edinburgh, and inserted in all the newspapers. Expresses were likewise despatched to Glasgow, Greenock, Paisley, Ayr, Perth, Dundee and Aberdeen—at all which places there were banks—to inform them of what was passing. The instant this resolution of paying no more specie was known in the street, a scene of confusion and uproar took place of which it is utterly impossible for those who did not witness it to form an idea.

" Our counting-house, and indeed the offices of all the banks, were instantly crowded to the door with people clamorously demanding payment in gold of their interest-receipts, and vociferating for silver in change of our circulating paper. It was in vain that we urged the order of Council—which, however, applied, merely to the Bank of England—and the general resolution adopted by all other banks in Edinburgh. They were deaf to every argument and although no symptom, nor indeed threatening of violence appeared, their noise, and the bustle they made, was intolerable ; which may be readily believed when it is considered that they were mostly of the lowest and most ignorant classes, such as fish-women, carmen, street porters and butcher's men, all bawling out at once for change, and jostling one another in their endeavours who should get nearest to the table, behind which were cashiers and ourselves endeavouring to pacify them as well as we could.

" Of our interest-receipts we were prompt in payment ; but instead of giving our own circulating notes, as heretofore, we paid the value in notes of the public banks . . . the sums had been deposited with us not in specie, but in such notes as we now gave back to the holders. With regard to our circulating notes . . . we felt the hardship on the holders, who were deprived of the means of purchasing with ready money the necessaries of life, as there were no notes of less value than twenty shillings and it was with the utmost difficulty they could get change anywhere else ; for the instant it was known that payments in specie were suspended, not a person would part with a single shilling that they could keep, and the consequence was that both gold and silver specie was hoarded up and instantly disappeared. . . . Saturday was the day on which we had the severest outcry to encounter . . . many master-tradesmen requested in the most earnest manner to have a little silver for enabling them to pay their workpeople. All we could do when sensible that their demand proceeded from *real* necessity, was privately to change a note or two by taking them into a separate room, for we durst not do it openly in the counting-house for fear of raising a riot.

" It was a matter of agreeable surprise to see in how short a time after the suspension of paying in specie, the run on us ceased. . . . It was remarkable, also after the first surprise and alarm was over, how quietly the country submitted, as they still do, to transact all business by means of bank notes for which the issuers give no specie as formerly. The wonder was the greater because the act of the Privy Council first, and afterwards the act of Parliament, applied merely, as I have already said, to the Bank of England, while all other banks, both in England and Scotland were left to carry on their business without any protection from Parliament."

Forbes adds in a footnote that no attempt had till then (he was writing in 1803) been made to force any Scotch bank to pay in specie ; nor to his knowledge had any similar attempt been made in England, except against Oakes & Son of Bury St. Edmunds by a Mr. Grigby, whose conduct was severely reprobated by Mr. Baron Hotham, who tried and apparently managed to shelve the case.

§ 2. INCONVERTIBLE PAPER

The crisis, with its excitement and alarm, eased the situation. Private expenditure, both for consumption and investment, was doubtless checked by the general consternation, and the Government now began to check it further by imposing additional taxation, which made it more difficult for the individual both to buy what he wanted and to save money out of his income. Even public expenditure was checked to some extent ; in the next four years it was rather less than in 1796, and then only rose slowly, so that in 1810 it was but 76¾ millions, while the revenue had risen to 67. The rake had suspended his progress, and there was no need of a depreciation of currency to square the account of aggregate produce and aggregate money expenditure. Cash payments might have been resumed after a few months, and the Bank was quite willing. But no government involved in a great war is willing to give up so potent an engine for surreptitiously fleecing its subjects as an inconvertible currency, whether in its own hands or in that of a bank which it influences. For " political reasons " the Restriction Act was continued.

Joined with the determination of the public to accept notes, the Act placed in the hands of the Bank the power of creating money without limit for the benefit of its shareholders, or Proprietors, as they were called. It could have lent notes to every one who offered one per cent. for an advance ; it could have bought up all the public funds except those belonging to the most careless or obstinate stockholders ; it could have subscribed the whole amount of every Government loan for the war. But the Directors had long managed the Bank with one eye indeed on the interest of the proprietors but with the other on that of the " monied interest " generally. The example of the assignats, just finishing their meteoric career in France, was sufficient to prevent them from adopting the fantastic belief of the cranks who believe that currency—alone among all objects of commerce—can be offered in indefinite quantity without depreciation of value. They recognized that to prevent eventual disaster to their class and country the issue of notes must be subject to limitation, and with their natural

conservatism they thought it sufficient to limit it
as they had limited it before the Restriction Act.
Now before the Restriction Act they had been in the
habit of making advances of notes whenever it seemed
safe to do so, and the issue of notes thus appeared to
be limited to the amount which could be advanced
with safety.   What could be better than to go on
being guided by this rule ?

They overlooked the fact that the conditions were
altered.   Before the Suspension the convertibility of
the notes absolutely prevented the Bank from increasing its issue whenever the value of a given quantity
of gold was appreciably greater than that of the notes
which promised to pay that quantity ; the Bank could
not lend additional notes promising to pay the bearer
on demand, say, £210 at a moment when any bearer
would find it profitable to demand the 200 golden
guineas to which he was entitled because he could sell
them for substantially more than £210.   At such a
moment more notes would be coming in than were
going out, and more gold going out than coming in,
and this would continue until parity was restored or
the Bank broken.   In order to continue doing as they
did before the Suspension, therefore, the Directors
should not only have considered the soundness of each
particular advance but should also have considered
how the whole position would have looked if the
Suspension had not been in force.   Had they done so,
they would clearly have limited advances and reduced
the amount of notes in circulation whenever £1 in notes
became worth appreciably less than $123\frac{1}{4}$ grains of
standard gold in the market—or, as it would commonly be expressed, whenever the price of gold rose appreciably above £3 17s. $10\frac{1}{2}d.$, and would have maintained
this policy until £1 in notes and $123\frac{1}{4}$ grains of gold
were again equal in value.

When a bank's advances of notes are unlimited
except by the lack of additional solvent borrowers,
they are certain in any long run to become greater

than when they are limited not only by that but also
by the necessity of keeping the notes up to the value
of the gold promised on their faces (see *Report*,
p. 50). The Bank of Ireland, put by the Irish Parliament under the same Restriction as the Bank of England, and adopting the same policy, caused an obvious
severance of the value of its notes from that of
the promised gold in a very short time. The Bank
of England, perhaps because of a higher standard
of security in the individual case, perhaps because
its stereotyped 5 per cent. rate was more deterrent to
borrowers in the circumstances of the time and country than the charge made by the Bank of Ireland,
moved more slowly. In the earlier years of the
Restriction such dealings in gold as were recorded,
the foreign exchanges, and the quantity of bullion
which the Bank managed to obtain and hold, all
indicate little discrepancy between the value of notes
and gold bullion. The pound sterling, in which all
transactions were calculated, was always worth less
than 123¼ grains of gold, but the difference was never
large enough to be important. In 1808, however,
owing, it is said, to the opening up of South America
to British commerce, a wave of optimism—called
"speculation" by contemporaries—among traders
caused an excessive rise in the price of many articles.
The Bank was prevented by the usury laws from at
once benefiting its Proprietors and moderating the
enthusiasm of the traders by raising its rate of discount, and, being by no means exempt from the
failings of the crowd, would probably not have done
so even if it had been able. Under convertibility a
check would have been imposed by the limited quantity of gold, which would eventually have made the
Bank "anxious for the safety of its establishment";
with the means of manufacturing unlimited amounts
of money on the premises, the Bank had no fears, and
"accommodated the public," perhaps not quite as
liberally as usual, though of that there is no evidence,

but at any rate too liberally to allow £1 to remain nearly equal in purchasing power to 123¼ grains of gold. Early in 1809 the price of gold went up to 90s., or to put it the other way £1 in notes would only buy about as much as 107 grains of gold instead of 123¼. The foreign exchanges told the same tale. On August 29 the first of three letters from Ricardo (reprinted for Johns Hopkins University, 1903) appeared in the *Morning Chronicle*. It begins with a statement that the present excess of the market price of gold over the mint price has excited much attention, but that the public " do not seem to be sufficiently impressed with the importance of the subject, nor of the disastrous consequences which may attend the further depreciation of paper," and goes on to explain, with a lucidity never surpassed in the author's later works, how the insufficient limitation of notes, due to their inconvertibility and the absence of any substituted check, had led to a difference between the value of £1 in notes and the 123¼ grains of gold to which £1 was formerly equal.

On February 1, 1810, Francis Horner, who till then had played no prominent part in Parliament, moved the House of Commons for various " accounts and returns respecting the present state of the circulating medium and the bullion trade," and said he intended to move for a committee to consider the subject. The Commitee was appointed on February 19 with the reference given at the head of the Report below (p. 3). The members, a list of whom will be found below on p. xlii. were largely experts. They took evidence on twenty-two days from Thursday, February 22, to March 26 ; on seven days from March 26 to April 18, and on May 22 and 25. Horner was Chairman, and the Minutes of Evidence show him to have occupied the Chair at all these meetings until March 15, after which, owing chiefly to his absence on circuit, he only presided at three of the meetings, Huskisson taking seven, Henry Thornton three, and Davies Giddy one. The Minutes of Evidence, like all others of the period, never attribute the questions asked to particular questioners : questions were doubtless supposed to be put by the Committee as a body, speaking by the mouth of the Chairman. That some at least of the questions were read out from slips of paper handed to the Chairman by members is suggested by the occasional appearance of questions beginning with the word " Whether," the words " please ask the witness " being no doubt understood if not actually prefixed.

In Horner's *Memoirs and Correspondence* (vol. ii. p. 47) there is a letter written on June 26, when the Report was still in the printer's hands, in which he says : " The Report is in truth very clumsily and prolixly drawn ; stating nothing but very old doctrines on the subject it treats of, and stating them in a more imperfect form than they have frequently appeared in before. It is a motley composition by Huskisson, Thornton, and myself; each having written parts which are tacked together without any care to give them an uniform style or a very exact connection. One great merit the Report, however, possesses ; that it declares, in very plain and pointed terms, both the true doctrine and the existence of a great evil growing out of the neglect of that doctrine. By keeping up the discussion, which I mean to do, and by forcing it on the attention of Parliament, we shall in time (I trust) effect the restoration of the old and only safe system."

A detailed summary of the Report is given below (p. xlvii.). Here it need only be said that what Horner calls its " true doctrine " was that when a paper currency originally founded on and convertible into coin has become inconvertible, it can only be kept up to its proper value by a limitation of its quantity based on observation of the price of bullion and the foreign exchanges. The " great evil growing out of neglect of that doctrine " was the gap between the value of £1 sterling (i.e. £1 in notes) and that of 123¼ grains of gold, as indicated by the price of gold and the foreign exchanges.

The Report assumes, without any attempt to prove, that the proper value of £1 at any time is the same as that of 123¼ grains of gold at that time. In view of the general belief that money ought to be stable in value, it was, strictly speaking, a mistake to assume this, since it may be alleged by an opponent that it is desirable that there should be a divergence between the value of £1 and that of 123¼ grains of gold if it happens that the value of the gold, measured in general purchasing power (such as is indicated by an index number of prices), undergoes some alteration. If, for example, gold will buy double or will only buy half as much of ordinary services and commodities as it bought down to a year or two ago, and as it will buy again after a year or two, there would be much to be said for an inconvertible currency which showed a considerable divergence from it, provided that the divergence indicated greater stability. So it could not be assumed straightway that the value of £1 in notes ought to be always the same as that of 123¼ grains of gold : the value of £1 in notes at any moment might be nearer the normal or ordinary value of £1 than the value of 123¼ grains was. But this was of no importance for the practical controversy then in hand, since then, as in most, if not all, modern wars, no one could possibly deny that gold had in fact varied *less* from its normal purchasing power than the paper currency. Prices, it was universally admitted, were much above their normal level : that is, £1 would buy much less than usual. The 123¼ grains of gold would also exchange for much less, but at any rate they would buy more than £1 in notes—you could get 90s. for an ounce, which is equal to 23s. 1d. for 123¼ grains, and 23s. 1d. must buy more than £1. All that the Bullion Committee need have claimed was that it was undesirable for the purchasing power (or " value ") of £1 to fall *below* that of 123¼ grains) of gold *at a time when the purchasing power (or " value ") of gold was admittedly—and with admittedly unsatisfactory results—itself much below the normal.* If the Committee had done this and avoided putting an unproved assumption in place of it, much confusion would have been avoided : but in the extreme infancy of the invention of price index numbers, so much could scarcely have been expected.

" The Report," says Smart in his *Annals,* p. 255, " was presented on the day previous (June 8) to the prorogation of Parliament, and could not, of course, be discussed. Copies in fact were not in the hands of members till the middle of August (the number of tables in the appendix having delayed the printing), but the substance and the recommenda- tion were circulated in the newspapers immediately after it was laid on the table. Its arguments were at once combated by a host of pamphlets ; its conclusions said to be inconsistent with the evi- dence ; and even the motives of its members questioned. In reply, Huskisson, who had been one of the most active members of the Committee, followed it up in October by an able pamphlet, entitled *The Question concerning the Depreciation of our Currency stated and examined*—restating and expanding the Report—which ran through several editions in a few months."

Davies Giddy, another prominent member of the Committee, attempted *A Plain Statement of the Bullion Question,* which is at least as successful as most modern efforts at elementary exposition on the subject. Malthus discussed the question with Ricardo in private conversation and correspondence, and wrote an article for the February *Edinburgh Review,* to which Ricardo replied in an Appendix to the fourth edition of his *High Price of Bullion* (see Ricardo's *Letters* to Malthus, p. 10, and Horner's *Memoirs,* vol. ii. p. 68). Horner, we may gather from his own and other speeches in the House of Commons on April 5, 1811, thought the Report would lose nothing by delay, and it was not till May 6 that he moved the House into Committee to consider it.

With what would now, at any rate, be regarded as very bad parliamentary strategy, though he says that it was recommended to him by parliamentary experts, he moved sixteen resolutions, all academic and only likely to raise unnecessary controversy except the fourteenth, which declared it to be the duty of the Bank to consider the foreign exchanges and the price of bullion in determining the amount of its issues so long as the Suspension continued, and the sixteenth, which pronounced it expedient that the Suspension should terminate, whether the war was at an end or not, in two years' time. A four days' debate took place, in which Horner spoke for three hours and was supported by Henry Thornton, Huskisson and five other members of his Committee and by Canning, whose speech he thought the best of all. The most doughty opponent was Rose, whose speech, however, is not reported in Hansard but merely copied from a printed version subsequently published by him. There were two divisions, the first of which rejected the theory of the resolutions by 151 to 75, and the second rejected the definite time limit for Suspension by 180 to 45.

On May 13 Vansittart, according to notice given in this debate, brought forward seventeen counter-resolutions modelled on Horner's, but taking the line that there was no divergence of value between notes and *coin*, and that the divergence between notes and coin on the one hand and bullion on the other was due not to superfluity of notes but to shortage of bullion, and was therefore quite proper. Owing to the failure of the Bullion Report to explain that the "evil" of the divergence of notes from coin lay in the fact that it made the prices of commodities more abnormal than they otherwise would be, this argument that the paper had the right value and gold the wrong value was never adequately dealt with ; Vansittart and his friends were not asked to explain why they thought the paper standard better than the gold standard, in which prices would have been appreciably lower than they were Vansittart himself in the sixteenth resolution admitted that the Suspension should terminate as soon as " the political and commercial relations of the country " rendered it " compatible with the public interest," which implies that the gold standard was better for ordinary times. The seventeenth resolution declared it " highly inexpedient and dangerous now to fix a definite period for the removal of the Restriction earlier than the existing limit of six months after the conclusion of peace." All the resolutions were carried on May 15 (Hansard, pp. 1–127, 134–46, 150–75).

The third of Vansittart's resolutions asserted that " the promissory notes of the Bank of England have hitherto been, and are, at this time, held in public estimation to be equivalent to the legal coin of the realm, and generally accepted as such in all transactions to which such coin is legally applicable." This equivalence was denied by several members in the debates, and Lord King, a descendant of Locke, who had written as early as 1803 a pamphlet to prove that notes were depreciated, resolved to give the lie to it. Before the Midsummer quarter-day he addressed a letter to his tenants saying that he could no longer accept notes in satisfaction of their contracts in their leases to pay " good and lawful money of Great Britain," and that he therefore required payment in guineas, or in an equal weight of Portuguese coin, or in notes sufficient to purchase an equal weight of standard gold at the market price of the day.

The effect of this was to compel Parliament to pass legislation which was equivalent to making bank notes legal tender, though there was a childish attempt to avoid doing it in so many words.

In November, 1810, the price of gold was down to 84s. 6d., but soon began to rise again, and in August, 1813, it attained the height of 110s., making the value of £1 in notes only equal to that of 87¼ grains of gold instead of 123¼. By October, 1814, the divergence had greatly diminished ; the price of gold had sunk to 85s. In February, 1815, just before the escape of Napoleon from Elba, it was a little higher, at 89s., and that event made it shoot up to 107s. After Waterloo it fell rapidly, and was only 83s. in October, 1815. In the next twelve months it fell to 78s. 6d., never again during the Suspension to rise above 83s. (*Lords' Committee on Resumption of Cash Payments;* 1819, App. C.1, in sessional vol. iii.: *Commons Committee on the Bank Charter* 1831-2, App. 96 in sessional vol. vi.)

Vansittart told the House of Commons on February 10, 1815, that everything that had happened since the beginning of the Bullion controversy went to show that Horner's doctrine was wrong. It must be admitted that the course of events from 1810, to 1816 was unfavourable to the easy propagation and acceptance of the doctrine, for from August, 1810, to August, 1813, while the Bank of England circulation did not increase at all, the price of gold was rising, and from August, 1813, to October, 1814, while the circulation rose 3½ millions the price of gold was falling. And the violent fluctuation in the price of gold in the year of Waterloo could certainly not be attributed to changes in the note circulation.

But economics resembles therapeutics in the difficulty of isolating causes. A patient is not justified in concluding that his doctor's prescription for him was wrong simply because he recovered from his illness without taking it. He might have recovered quicker if he had ; or a change of weather, habits or diet may have acted as an effective substitute. So here the defender of the Report may effectively reply to Vansittart and his supporters that if the Bank had "adverted to" the price of gold and the foreign exchanges in regulating its issue, and consequently been stiffer in giving advances, and so reduced its issue from 1810 to 1813, the price of gold would not have gone up, and the price of commodities in general would have fallen faster than it actually did. Commodities were falling in consequence of the diminution of readiness to buy—to part with money—characteristic of the reaction after a boom or period of "speculation," and the Bank by maintaining its circulation undiminished made the fall less than it would have been if the circulation had been contracted.

Supposing the Bank had adopted this policy with its eyes open, it might be defended on the ground that though it was desirable that prices should come down from the abnormal height of 1810, it was not desirable that they should come down with too much of a rush. Unfortunately for this defence, however, the diminution of the rapidity of the fall from 1810 to 1813 only aggravated the precipitousness of the fall at the end of the war. That fall, like other falls at the ends of wars in face of a currency stationary in amount, was caused in the first place by the sharp drop in public expenditure (just as the rise at the beginning of a war is caused by the opposite) and was maintained by the increased ease of obtaining ordinary commodities (from the price of which we form our idea of general prices). It was bound to take place unless the paper currency had been enormously increased, like that of some countries after the war of 1914–18, and this not being attempted, it would clearly have been better to have let prices down more rapidly between 1810 and 1813.

About the effect of the Napoleonic escapade of 1815, it may be recalled that the Report expressly confines the application of its theory to "any considerable period of time" (p. 45). It certainly does not ask us to believe that each sharp fluctuation of the comparative value of notes and gold shown either by the price of gold or the foreign exchanges was caused by alterations in the circulation of notes.

Any one who is puzzled by the fact that although when some other standard is established, gold "is only a commodity," yet the price (in notes) of gold does not always vary in the same proportion or even in the same direction as general prices (in notes), must be reminded that it is not necessary for the price of *each* commodity to vary in the same proportion and direction as the price of *all* commodities taken together. Each has its own set of special circumstances, and the special circumstances of gold were by no means unimportant. For one thing, it was still current as money over a wide area; for another, its production and movement was less interrupted by warlike operations than those of most articles of commerce; for a third it was more subject to being locked up in hoards at one time and poured out of hoards at another.

On the whole we may condemn Vansittart's theory as being as unsound as his financial administration was feeble.

§ 3. Resumption of Payment

After October, 1816, with the price of gold at 78s. 6d., only 7½d. above the coinage par, Resumption of Cash Payments should have seemed easy of attainment. But the Bank had found itself comfortable under the Suspension, and felt no enthusiasm for a return to a system which did not guarantee it against being asked to pay its debts at a possibly inconvenient moment ; and the Government and Parliament were as slack as they usually are after a great war. Moreover the quantity of coin likely to be required for the circulation was enormously overrated, so that a belief prevailed that the Bank would have to accumulate an enormous stock of coin (or bullion ready to be made into coin) before it could safely undertake once more to fulfil the promise (which it had continued throughout the Suspension to make on every note) to pay the bearer on demand such and such number of pounds. Now from February, 1808, to February, 1815, the Bank's "treasure," as its stock of gold and silver bullion and coin was often conveniently called, had fallen very steadily from nearly 8 to very little over 2 millions. The Directors set to work to increase the amount, and for some time were even willing to pay 80s. an ounce for gold for the purpose, which was much the same as giving £1 0s. 6d. each for sovereigns. It does not seem to have occurred to them that their promises to pay £1 being at the moment worth less than a sovereign, and being certain to be worth as much as a sovereign when Resumption took place, it would be much better to apply their resources to buying in and cancelling their promises to pay. If they had means to buy gold, they obviously had the means to cancel their notes at once, and it would clearly be better to do so at once, and pay £1, than to lay up the means of cancelling them in the future at the cost of £1 0s. 6d. In short it could not possibly be good policy to give forty-one promises to pay £1 and get in exchange what would soon only suffice to redeem forty of these promises. But this is a truth which many authorities fail to see even now, when they advocate the accumulation of a backing to depreciated inconvertible paper instead of asking for the reduction of the paper.

In November, 1816, the price of gold being then 78s. 6d., and the treasure probably over 8 millions, the Directors decided to find out by experiment how much coin the public was likely to ask for on Resumption. In accordance with a provision which had been in the Restriction Acts ever since 1797, they gave notice to the Speaker that they intended on and after December 2, 1816, to pay gold on demand to all holders of notes for £1 and £2 dated earlier than 1812. Very few notes were presented in response to the invitation ; the Directors were encouraged to go further, and in April, 1817, the price of gold being 79s. and the treasure probably over 10 millions, they offered repayment in gold on and after May 2 to all holders of £1 and £2 notes dated earlier than 1816. As this too evoked little response and their treasure was near 12 millions, they gave notice in September, 1817, although the price of gold had now risen to 80s., that they would on and after October 1 repay in gold all notes of every denomination issued before January 1, 1817. Their failure to " advert to the price of bullion and the foreign exchanges " on this occasion had its natural effect. Melting and exportation being now profitable, large amounts of notes were sent in for redemption : the depletion was only gradual, presumably owing to the law against export preventing more than a dribble of coin and bullion outwards. Between August, 1817, and February, 1819, the treasure fell 7½ millions ; we might expect to find the notes also reduced by that amount, and if they had been, the decrease of notes and the increase, outside the Bank, of gold might well have brought gold and notes to a parity in the market. But while repaying the pre-1817 dated notes, the Bank must have been counteracting the effect of that action by issuing additional new (and still inconvertible) notes, for while the treasure diminished by 7½ millions, the total of notes diminished by only 4½. About half the difference of 3 millions is accounted for by a greater excess of "securities," public and private, over deposits, and the remainder by a diminution of the Rest or undivided profit which was the consequence of a transaction entered into by the Government and the Bank in 1816. In that year the Bank, which had been steadily increasing its "Rest" for nine years till it stood at over 8½ millions, capitalised nearly 3 millions of this undivided profit, lending the amount (like the whole of. its previous capital) permanently to the State at 3 per cent., and in subsequent years it continued to pay its dividend at the usual 10 per cent., which meant paying its Proprietors nearly £300,000 per annum more than they had been receiving in 1807–15. Now in fact a reduction of the Bank's profits which took place after the war—and which surely could have been foreseen—called for a smaller rather than a larger distribution. The joint action of the loan, the larger distribution, and the smaller profits was to cause the Rest to fall from £8,640,000 at February, 1816, to £5,192,000 in February, 1819, and further to £3,521,000 in February, 1821, which greatly helps to explain the astonishing feebleness of the Bank at this important period of its history.

Early in 1819 secret committees were appointed by both Lords and Commons to consider the whole question of Resumption. Almost immediately both Committees sent in *interim* reports to the effect that the "partial resumption" attempted by the Bank with the exchanges unfavourable was folly and must be stopped. Parliament accordingly inhibited the Bank from going on with it.

But what was to be done? It was all very well for supporters of the Bullion Report to recommend reduction of issue, but how could the Bank reduce

to any considerable extent? In the palmy days
of 1810, when the average amount of commercial
bills discounted was 20 millions, the Bank could
be blamed for not allowing this amount to reduce
itself and cancelling notes as they came in. But
in 1817 and 1818 the commercial bills were under
4½ millions. The whole of Private Securities
amounted to little more than 9 millions in February,
1819, and this was double what it had averaged
in the two preceding half-yearly accounts. Whether
notes were to be substantially reduced or a large
sum of treasure acquired, it was obvious that the
one considerable debtor to the Bank, that is, the
State, must repay a large portion of what was
under Public Securities. Accordingly both Committees and Parliament agreed to the request of
the Bank that 10 millions of Exchequer Bills held
by it should be paid off. The result of this, coupled
with changes of quite minor importance, was that
the Bank, instead of defeating itself by buying gold
with additions to its note-issue, was able to accumulate a great quantity of the treasure which it supposed to be required, while at the same time making
that small reduction in the note issue, which, as
Ricardo had always contended, was all that was
necessary. At the end of February, 1821, the
circulation was 19 per cent. less than it had been at
the highest point (August 1817), while the treasure
was a little greater than it was then and 8½ millions
above the low point of August, 1819, though the
Bank had not paid more than the coinage price for
the addition. (See Table II. p. xliv. below.)

It is not surprising that even the Bank then
thought it safe to resume cash payments; it could
have paid off in metal half of its note-issue, and
the remainder would have been only about equal
to the amount which it was able to keep in circulation thirty years earlier, before suspension was
ever thought of. An elaborate arrangement sug-

gested by Ricardo as far back as 1811 in the Appendix
to his *High Price of Bullion a proof of the depreciation of bank notes*, had been made by Parliament
on the recommendation of the Committees.   Under
this the Bank was for a time to have paid in big
ingots of bullion only, first at the rate of an ounce
to 81s., then to 79s. 6d., and lastly at the coinage
rate of 77s. 10½d. before beginning to pay in coin
on May 1, 1823.   The end was hastened by agree-
ment between the Bank and Parliament, and full
Resumption took place on May 1, 1821.

Scarcely any diminution of the treasure took place.

Almost, if not quite, to the last, the Bank officially,
at any rate, denied the doctrine of the Bullion
Report.   On March 25, 1819, the Court of Directors
could not "refrain from adverting to an opinion,
strongly insisted on by some, that the Bank has
only to reduce its issues to obtain a favourable
turn in the exchanges and a consequent influx of
the precious metals," and conceived "it to be its
duty to declare that it is unable to discover any
solid foundation for such a sentiment" (*Commons
Secret Committee on Resumption*, 1819, p. 263).
But in 1827 this resolution was rescinded on the
motion of a Director, who, five years later, was
able to say of the opinion "that the Bank should
conduct itself, in its issues, with reference to the
state of the foreign exchanges and the bullion
market," that he did not "think there was one
person in the Bank of England that denies it or is
disposed to act in opposition to it" (*Bank-Charter
Committee, Evidence*, vol. vi. of 1831–2, qq. 2072–7).

§ 4. MORAL

We may well conclude by asking how it was that
Horner's "great evil" (above, p. xxii.) did not grow
much greater than it did.   Why was not the incon-

vertible currency increased much above the very
moderate amount which it actually attained ?

Tooke ascribes the moderation of the issue throughout simply to the 5 per cent. rate charged by the
Bank, which he says was a high rate in the circumstances of the time (*History of Prices*, vol. i. p. 161).
Doubtless additional money always put on the
market by way of loan would be kept from flowing
in a very large stream if the issuer charged a very
high rate of interest for it.　A man with an inexhaus-
tible goldmine workable without expense in his
cellar would not issue enough to bring down the
value of gold appreciably if he did not sell his gold
(or coin and spend it, which is the same thing)
and refused to lend it except at 20 per cent. interest.
But even if 5 per cent. was sufficiently high to be
a nearly adequate check throughout the most of
the period and quite adequate after the end of the
war, that will not explain the moderation of the
issue, inasmuch as the Directors could at any
moment, if they had chosen, reduce the rate to
4 or less.　Some few years after the Resumption
they did so reduce it ; why did they not do so
during the Suspension ?　Moreover, it is not the
fact that lending at 5 per cent. was the only means
the Bank used for issuing its notes : it often lent
them to the Government at lower rates, and it paid
them away for any property or securities which it
bought.　The fixed, or rather customary, rate of
discount at 5 per cent. hindered but did not absolutely preclude the issue of unlimited amounts of
notes.

The solution seems to be this.　In the earlier
part and again during the last part of the Suspension,
the Directors expected Resumption to take place
very soon ; and this naturally led them to act as
if it were necessary that the Bank should be " strong "
in the sense of easily able to meet its liabilities in
gold if required to do so, and strength in this sense

was clearly incompatible with reckless issue. In the early years of the Suspension moderation was made easier by the Government's demands on the Bank being held in check by the alarm which the crisis of 1797 had created in the minds of ministers who knew what had happened to the assignats in France. In the post-war period, while the conduct of the Government was much less creditable, Resumption was a more insistent monitor.

In the middle period, after the failure of the Peace of Amiens had accustomed men's minds to the idea of perpetual war, and the spectre of Resumption faded away, the Directors did become somewhat slacker, but they were sharply pulled up by the criticism to which they were subjected in the Bullion controversy. For in spite of all their protestations that the currency was not excessive and that the doctrine of the Bullion Report was without foundation, there is good reason to believe that they were to some important extent influenced by it.

In the first place it seems *primâ facie* altogether improbable that the Bank Directors could fail to be to some extent influenced in the direction of caution by all the criticism of the Report and parliamentary debates, and equally improbable that some at least of the twenty-four would not only feel that their Governor and Deputy-Governor had made out a poor case before the Committee, (see *Report*, pp. 32–4, 46–8) but also be inclined to doubt whether, after all, there was not " something in " the idea that the price of gold and the exchanges must be considered in determining how much to advance.

Secondly, even in the parliamentary debates on the Report there are some indications of a change of opinion in the Bank. Embedded in the vast mass of unimportant matter of which Rose's speech is composed, there is a parenthesis of considerable interest. " I am desirous here of saying a word

in extenuation of answers given suddenly on points
on which witnesses have not been previously apprised
that they were to be examined upon : I mean that
if the Governor and Deputy-Governor had been
apprised of the question respecting their discounting
at a low interest, they would have given a different
answer ; which I am led to believe from a conversation with the former." (*Hansard*, May, 1811, p.
863.) This retractation by the Governor refers to the
evidence (part of which is quoted on p. 48 of the
Report) in which the Governor, supported by the
Deputy-Governor, who was before the Committee
at the same time, contended that the requirement
of good security in each individual case would be
a sufficient limitation of the issue of notes, however
low the rate of discount might be.   Rose failed to
see that the withdrawal made it impossible to claim,
as the Bank had claimed, that the regulation of the
inconvertible currency was automatic, requiring
no exercise of judgment on the part of the Directors.
It amounted to an admission that the rate of discount might be too low to limit advances sufficiently,
in which case the Directors' duty would be to raise
it, or if that were impossible owing to the maximum
legal rate of interest (fixed at 5 per cent. by a statute
of Anne) being already reached, to add some further
check : in either case they would have to exercise
their judgment on the question whether the total
of advances required further limitation or not, and
Rose and his friends were as unable as the Governor
to suggest any criterion other than that proposed
by the Bullion Committee.   Henry Thornton's
brother Samuel, who was as well entitled to speak
for the Bank as any one, having been Director for
over thirty years (he was in office from 1780–1833),
also seems to have been inclined to jettison the
Governor's answer, as *Hansard* says (p. 1163) he
" disclaimed the idea that the Bank issued paper
to an unlimited amount.   Every one of the twenty-

four gentlemen at its head had a vote whether each sum was or was not too high." This distinctly admits that the total of advances was not beyond the control of the Directors : they were obliged to exercise their judgment about it, and it is certainly difficult to see how they could do so without directly or indirectly being consciously or unconsciously influenced by, or "adverting to," as the phrase was, the price of bullion and the exchanges.

The effect of the report is suggested much less strongly by the mere inspection of the total of notes in circulation than by an examination of the details which account for that total. The Directors, with some justice, always contended that they had little control over the issue so far as it was occasioned by the demands of the Government, and wished to be judged by their policy in regard to discounts, so that whether they were on the restrictive or the expansive tack is to be decided chiefly by their control over " private securities," and especially over that portion of this item which consisted of commercial bills discounted. Now the Bank would not give the Bullion Committee a plain statement of the annual amount of this last item, and would not allow them to publish the " scale " which it did furnish, showing only the percentage increases from year to year (See *Report* below, pp. 56–7). The actual figures were obtained by the Bank-Charter Committee of 1832 and are given in Table II. below. It is not surprising that the Bullion Committee were much impressed by the " scale " and that the Bank did not care to publish the fact that the average amount of commercial paper under discount had increased from under 3 millions in 1795 and just over 3½ in 1796 to 15½ in 1809. In 1810, the year of the Bullion Report, it was further up to over 20 millions, after which it fell like a stone to £14,355,000 in 1811, £14,292,000 in 1812, and £12,330,000 in 1813, which is actually less than it was in any of the four years preceding the Bullion

Report. After recovering to 15 millions in 1815, it collapsed altogether, being in 1817 lower than in any previous year since the Suspension. Of course the rise immediately before 1810 and the fall immediately after were due chiefly to the " speculation " and depression after the speculation on which Tooke insists, and the later collapse was due to the end of the war, but it is scarcely credible that the Directors would not have withstood with greater success this enormous diminution in the cream of their business if they had been as impervious to the teachings of the Report as they professed themselves to be.

Whatever may be the precise explanation, there can in these days be no doubt that the experiment of entrusting what no community should entrust to any institution, the power of creating money without limit, to the Bank of England compares very favourably with the modern plan of entrusting it to the Government itself or to a State bank completely under the control of the Government. In the comparatively short war of 1914–18 currencies " not convertible at will into a coin which is exportable " (*Report*, p. 17) were issued by Governments and Government banks in amounts compared with which the 100 per cent. increase in thirteen years, which made the Bullion Committee complain so vigorously in 1810, looks absolutely trifling. The British Government brought out an entirely new issue of £1 and 10s. notes and increased it to 293 millions at the date of the armistice : the Bank of France increased its issue from 6,000 million francs to 30,500 millions : the Italian increase was from 2,500 millions to over 8,000. The precise increase in Germany and Austria-Hungary is obscure but understood to have been much greater. The record since the armistice is still less of a kind to give the present day Europeans ground for boasting themselves better than their fathers. In twenty-three weeks

the British Government had increased the note
issue by 59 millions more, and the total still stood
on October 1, 1919, at 335 millions. The French issue
on October 2 was 36,250 millions, the Italian in July
1919 was about 10,000 millions and the Russian
rouble is being manufactured in numbers which
suggest astronomers' calculations rather than anything terrestrial.

The result is what Horner and the Bullion Committee feared. The pound in October 1919 will buy
just about the same amount of gold as it would
when the Bullion Committee sat in 1810, that is,
about 107 grains instead of the normal 123¼, but
it is respectable compared with its colleagues in
Europe : the franc will buy about 3½ instead of
nearly 5 grains : the case of the lira is rather worse ;
the mark will buy little more than 1 grain instead
of 6 ; the Austrian krone and the Russian rouble
are worse. Politicians have certainly egregiously
failed to "advert to the foreign exchanges and
the price of bullion in regulating their issues " :
instead they amuse their ignorant subjects with
fantastic explanations of the perversity of the exchanges and chimerical schemes for "correcting"
them by stopping imports or borrowing still more
from abroad.

No one can contend that these paper standards
are superior to the gold standard. In the first
place they are all different, and in the second the
one common property that they possess in all making
prices much higher than they would be if paper and
gold had not diverged, marks them as all inferior.
Gold has been produced in almost the usual quantities throughout the war, it is almost alone among
metals in not having been used in the manufacture
of munitions of war, and it has been thrown out of
currency use over a wide area. Consequently it
is greatly depreciated as against commodities : that
is, 123¼ grains of gold or any freely exportable gold

coin will buy far less of ordinary commodities than before the war—perhaps scarcely half. Consequently each of the particular local divergencies between paper and gold simply constitutes a local aggravation of a world-wide rise of prices, a great part of which is itself produced by the general introduction of the paper currencies.

When the scales at last fall from the eyes of the people of Europe, groaning under the rise of prices, they will no longer cry to their Governments " Hang the profiteers ! " but " Burn your paper money, and go on burning it till it will buy as much gold as it used to do ! "

It only remains to add here a few details which could not be conveniently introduced into the sketch given above.

The Bullion Report was, of course, originally printed in the usual parliamentary folio (in vol. III. of 1810, which includes also the reports of the 1797 Lords Secret Committee on the Bank and of the 1804 Commons Committee on the Irish Currency frequently referred to by the Bullion Committee). The Report itself occupies 33 pages, the Minutes of Evidence 118, and the appendix of Accounts and Tables 81. Though it was only published in August, it was out of print by November (Horner's *Memoirs*, vol. II. p. 59), and an octavo edition dated 1810 was published by J. Johnson and Co. in which the Report occupies 78 pages, the Evidence 237 in smaller print, and the Accounts 115 in very small print. This is much more often met with than the original folio edition, and it is therefore hoped that readers who wish to consult the evidence will be assisted by the fact that it has been followed in the present reprint of the Report, so that the page-references to the Evidence are to it and not to the folio edition.

(If necessary, they can easily be converted into almost exact references to the folio by dividing them by 2 and adding 33 to the result.) The printers of the octavo show intelligence on p. 47 by suggesting that "security" in the folio should be amended to "scarcity," which is certainly true.

The list of members of the Committee given in the octavo edition is defective in not containing Charles Long, Joint Paymaster of the Forces, who was appointed, as the Journals of the House of Commons record, as an additional member on March 12, and who distinguished himself by being the only member of the Committee who spoke against its report in the Commons debate. Twelve of the members have obtained admission to that rather wide-open temple of fame, the Dictionary of National Biography. These are Alexander Baring, J. Leslie Forster, Davies Giddy (vice Rose, who declined), Pascoe Grenfell, Francis Horner, W. Huskisson, H. Parnell, Rt. Hon. Spencer Perceval, R. Sharp, Rt. Hon. R. B. Sheridan, G. Tierney, and Henry Thornton : the other ten are Hon. J. Abercrombie, T. Brand, W. Dickinson, J. Irving, G. Johnstone, Charles Long, D. M. Magens, W. Manning, Earl Temple, and Thomas Thompson.

If it be asked who was the "very eminent Continental Merchant" (p. 19) "intimately acquainted with the trade between this Country and the Continent" (p. 25), the answer is that in the Evidence he, alone among the witnesses, appears as "Mr.—— a Continental Merchant." Ricardo, who says that one of his answers led the Committee (p. 5) to put the exchange with Hamburg at 9 per cent. below par when it was really 17 below, refers to him as "Mr. —— " simply (Works, p. 322, and p. 311 note). An obvious conjecture is that this modest Mr. Blank was the great N. M. Rothschild.

The two tables which follow will, it is hoped, elucidate both parts of the present volume.

TABLE I. VARIOUS STATISTICS

	Kingdom of Great Britain and Ireland.			Jevons' index number of prices. 1782 as 100.	Bank of England.	
	Expenditure.	Revenue.	Excess expended (col. i. less col. ii.)		Average amount of commercial bills under discount. Million £.	Average amount of public deposits. Million £.
1792	17·4	19·3	−1·9	93		
1793	24·2	19·8	4·4	99		
1794	29·6	20·2	9·4	98		
1795	51·7	19·9	31·8	117	2·9	
1796	57·7	21·5	36·2	125	3·5	
1797	50·5	23·1	27·4	110	5·3	
1798	50·9	31·0	19·9	118	4·5	
1799	55·4	35·6	19·8	130	5·4	
1800	56·5	34·1	22·4	141	6·4	
1801	60·6	34·1	26·5	153	7·9	
1802	49·5	36·4	13·1	119	7·5	
1803	49·0	38·6	10·4	128	10·7	
1804	58·6	46·2	12·4	122	10·0	
1805	66·9	50·9	16·0	136	11·4	
1806	68·5	55·8	12·7	133	12·4	
1807	67·3	59·3	8·0	132	13·5	12·7
1808	73·0	63·0	10·0	149	13·0	11·8
1809	76·5	63·7	12·8	161	15·5	11·1
1810	76·8	67·1	9·7	164	20·1	12·0
1811	83·6	65·2	18·4	147	14·4	10·2
1812	86·2	65·0	21·2	148	14·3	10·4
1813	105·4	68·7	36·7	149	12·3	10·4
1814	106·3	71·1	35·2	153	13·3	12·2
1815	92·1	72·2	19·9	132	14·9	11·7
1816	64·8	62·3	2·5	109	11·4	10·8
1817	53·5	52·0	1·5	120	4·0	8·7
1818	51·7	53·7	−2·0	135	4·3	7·1
1819	52·2	52·6	−0·4	117	6·5	4·5
1820	52·4	54·3	−1·9	106	3·9	3·7
1821	53·0	55·8	−2·8	94	2·7	3·9

For note to this table see page xlv.

TABLE II. BANK OF ENGLAND, 1792–1821

Year and month.	1 Notes in circulation.	2 Deposits	3 Rest.	4 Coin and bullion.	5 Private Securities.	6 Public Securities.	7 Col. 6 less col. 2 see note.
1792 F	11·3	5·5	2·7	6·5	3·1	9·9	4·4
A	11·0	5·5	2·7	5·4	3·2	10·7	5·2
1793 F	11·9	5·3	2·8	4·0	6·5	9·5	4·2
A	10·9	6·4	2·8	5·3	4·4	10·4	4·0
1794 F	10·7	7·9	2·9	7·0	4·6	10·0	2·1
A	10·3	5·9	3·0	6·8	3·6	8·9	3·0
1795 F	14·0	6·0	2·9	6·1	3·6	13·2	7·2
A	10·9	8·2	3·1	5·1	3·7	13·3	5·1
1796 F	10·7	5·7	3·2	2·5	4·2	13·0	7·3
A	9·2	6·7	3·2	2·1	6·2	10·9	4·2
1797 F	9·7	4·9	3·4	1·1	5·1	11·7	6·8
A	11·1	7·8	3·5	4·1	9·5	8·8	1·0
1798 F	13·1	6·1	3·4	5·8	5·6	11·2	5·1
A	12·2	8·3	3·4	6·5	6·4	10·9	2·6
1799 F	13·0	8·1	3·5	7·6	5·5	11·5	3·4
A	13·4	7·6	2·9	7·0	7·5	9·5	1·9
1800 F	16·8	7·1	3·7	6·1	7·4	14·0	6·9
A	15·0	8·3	3·9	5·2	8·6	13·6	5·3
1801 F	16·2	10·7	4·1	4·6	10·5	16·0	5·3
A	14·6	8·1	3·9	4·3	10·3	11·9	3·8
1802 F	15·2	6·9	4·1	4·2	7·8	14·2	7·3
A	17·1	9·7	4·2	3·9	13·6	13·5	3·8
1803 F	15·3	8·1	4·3	3·8	14·5	9·4	1·3
A	16·0	9·8	4·7	3·6	13·6	13·3	3·5
1804 F	17·1	8·7	4·6	3·4	12·3	14·7	6·0
A	17·2	9·7	4·8	5·9	10·8	15·0	5·3
1805 F	17·9	12·1	4·6	5·9	11·8	16·9	4·8
A	16·4	14·0	5·0	7·6	16·4	11·4	−2·6
1806 F	17·7	10·0	4·9	6·0	11·8	14·8	4·8
A	21·0	9·6	5·0	6·2	15·3	14·2	4·6
1807 F	17·0	11·8	4·8	6·1	14·0	13·5	1·7
A	19·7	11·8	5·0	6·5	16·5	13·4	1·6
1808 F	18·2	12·0	5·1	7·9	13·2	14·1	2·1
A	17·1	13·0	5·1	6·0	14·3	15·0	2·0
1809 F	18·5	10·0	5·1	4·5	14·4	14·7	4·7
A	19·6	12·3	5·3	3·7	18·1	15·3	3·0
1810 F	21·0	12·5	5·4	3·5	21·1	14·3	1·8
A	24·8	13·6	5·8	3·2	23·8	17·2	3·6

TABLE II—*Continued*

Year and month.	1 Notes in circulation	2 Deposits.	3 Rest.	4 Coin and bullion.	4 Private Securities.	6 Public Securities.	7 Col. 6 less col. 2 see note.
1811 F	23·4	11·4	5·7	3·4	19·9	17·2	5·8
A	23·3	11·1	6·0	3·2	15·2	21·9	10·8
1812 F	23·4	11·6	6·0	3·0	15·9	22·1	10·5
A	23·0	11·8	6·4	3·1	17·0	21·2	9·4
1813 F	23·2	11·3	6·3	2·9	12·9	25·0	13·7
A	24·8	11·2	6·8	2·7	14·5	25·6	14·4
1814 F	24·8	12·5	6·9	2·2	18·4	23·6	11·1
A	28·4	14·8	7·2	2·1	13·4	35·0	20·2
1815 F	27·3	11·7	7·6	2·0	17·0	27·5	15·8
A	27·2	12·7	8·3	3·4	20·7	24·2	11·5
1816 F	27·0	12·4	8·6	4·6	24·0	19·4	7·0
A	26·8	11·9	6·2	7·6	11·2	26·1	14·2
1817 F	27·4	10·8	5·7	9·7	8·7	25·5	14·7
A	29·5	9·1	5·6	11·7	5·5	27·1	18·0
1818 F	27·8	8·0	5·2	10·1	4·0	26·9	18·9
A	26·2	7·9	4·6	6·4	5·1	27·3	19·4
1819 F	25·1	6·4	4·1	4·2	9·1	22·4	16·0
A	25·3	6·3	3·8	3·6	6·3	25·4	19·1
1820 F	23·5	4·1	3·5	4·9	4·5	21·7	17·6
A	24·3	4·4	3·3	8·2	4·7	19·2	14·8
1821 F	23·9	5·6	3·2	11·9	4·8	16·0	10·4
A	20·3	5·8	3·6	11·2	2·7	15·8	10·0

NOTE TO TABLE I.

Cols. 1 and 2, Expenditure and Revenue, are taken from the 4th Report of the Commons' Committee on Public Income and Expenditure, 1828 (vol. v. of that session), Apps. Nos. 13, 14, 15. Col. 2 includes besides " ordinary Revenue " certain " other receipts " such as voluntary contributions and repayments of monies advanced for relief of merchants and other public objects. Col. 1 includes monies advanced for the same purposes, and also money raised for Austria £4,600,000 in 1795.

Col. 3 is obtained by deducting the amounts in col. 2 from those in col. 1, so that it shows how much money the State required to raise by some form of borrowing; the total is, of course, much smaller than the addition to the national debt made during the period, on account of the practice of raising loans in stock paying a low rate of interest and therefore issued at a very large discount.

Col. 4 is taken from Jevons' *Investigations in Currency and Finance*, p. 144. It relates to the actual prices in pounds sterling. Jevons gives another column in which he corrects these to allow for the depreciation of the paper pound, but it is not possible to deduce from the fact that the price of gold is 25 per cent. more than it would be if paper were convertible, that prices would be at that moment less exactly in that proportion. All that can be safely said is that they would be less.

Col. 5, Commercial paper under Discount, is from the Report of the Bank Charter Committee 1831–2 (in vol. vi. of that session), App. No. 59.

Col. 6, average aggregate amount of public deposits, is from the same, App. No. 24. The Committee asked for figures from 1800, but the Bank returned the reply : " The Bank is unable to furnish correctly the aggregate amounts of Public Deposits previous to the year 1807 : the Public Accounts prior to that period not being required generally to be kept at the Bank, and many public accounts at that time were in the names of individuals, without reference to that part cf the Public Service to which the Accounts applied."

NOTE TO TABLE II.

The figures are from the Bank-Charter Committee's Report, 1831–2, Appendix No. 5. The figures of the average of Public Deposits given in Table I., last col., show that from 1807–1821, and especially in the earlier years of that period, private deposits must have been almost negligible, and suggest that throughout the war we should probably get a better estimate of the fluctuations in the assistance rendered to Government by the Bank if we took the figures of Public Securities *less* the whole of Deposits than by simply accepting the figures of public securities as they stand. It is done in the last column of the table above, which contains the excess of col. 6 over col. 2.

SUMMARY OF THE REPORT

INTRODUCTION

SECTION III

CONTROL OF THE NOTE ISSUE

SECTION IV

INCREASE AND PRESENT AMOUNT OF PAPER IN CIRCULATION

REPORT

FROM

THE SELECT COMMITTEE

ON THE

HIGH PRICE OF BULLION

Ordered by The House of Commons to be Printed
8th June, 1810

Reprinted 1919

THE SELECT COMMITTEE appointed to enquire into the Cause of the High Price of GOLD BULLION, and to take into consideration the State of the CIRCULATING MEDIUM, and of the EXCHANGES between Great Britain and Foreign Parts ;—and to report the same, with their Observations thereupon, from time to time, to The House ;—HAVE, pursuant to the Orders of The House, examined the matters to them referred ; and have agreed to the following REPORT :

YOUR Committee proceeded, in the first instance, to ascertain what the price of Gold Bullion had been, as well as the rates of the Foreign Exchanges, for some time past ; particularly during the last year.

Your Committee have found that the price of Gold Bullion, which, by the regulations of His Majesty's Mint, is £3 17s. 10½d per ounce of standard fineness, was, during the years 1806, 1807 and 1808, as high as £4 in the market. Towards the end of 1808 it began to advance very rapidly, and continued very high during the whole year 1809 ; the market price of standard Gold in bars fluctuating from £4 9s. to £4 12s. per oz. The market price at £4 10s. is about 15½ per cent. above the Mint price.

Your Committee have found, that during the three first months of the present year, the price of standard Gold in bars remained nearly at the same price as during last year ; viz, from £4 10s. to £4 12s. per oz. In the course of the months of March and April, the price of standard Gold is quoted but once in Wettenhall's tables ; viz. on the 6th of April last, at £4 6s. which is rather more than 10 per cent. above the Mint price. The last quotations of the price of Gold, which have been given in those tables, are upon the 18th and 22nd of May, when Portugal Gold in coin is quoted at £4 11s. per oz. : Portugal Gold coin is about the same fineness as our standard. It is stated in the same tables, that in the month of March last, the price of new Doubloons rose from £4 7s. to £4 9s. per oz. Spanish Gold is from 4½ to 4¾ grains better than standard, making about 4s. per oz. difference in value.

It appears by the Evidence, that the price of foreign Gold coin is generally higher than that of bar Gold, on account of the former finding a more ready vent in foreign markets. The difference between Spanish and Portugal Gold in coin and Gold in bars, has of late been about 2s. per ounce. Your Committee have also to state, that there is said to be at present a difference of between 3s. and 4s. per ounce between the price of bar Gold which may be sworn off for exportation as being foreign Gold, and the price of such bar Gold as the Dealer will not venture to swear off ; while the former was about £4 10s. in the market, the latter is said to have been about £4 6s. On account of these extrinsic differences, occasioned either by the expense of coinage, or by the obstructions of law, the price of standard Gold in bars, such as may be exported, is that which it is most material to keep generally in view through the present enquiry.

It appeared to Your Committee, that it might be of use, in judging of the cause of this high price of Gold Bullion, to be informed also of the prices of Silver during the same period. The price of standard Silver in His Majesty's Mint is 5s. 2d. per ounce ; at this standard price, the value of a Spanish Dollar is 4s. 4d. or, which comes to the same thing, Spanish Dollars are, at that standard price, worth 4s. 11½d. per ounce. It is stated in Wettenhall's tables, that throughout the year 1809, the price of new Dollars fluctuated from 5s. 5d. to 5s. 7d. per ounce, or from 10 to 13 per cent. above the Mint price of standard Silver. In the course of the last month, new Dollars have been quoted as high as 5s. 8d. per ounce, or more than 15 per cent, above the Mint price.

Your Committee have likewise found, that towards the

end of the year 1808, the Exchanges with the Continent became very unfavourable to this Country, and continued still more unfavourable through the whole of 1809, and the three first months of the present year.

Hamburgh, Amsterdam, and Paris, are the principal places with which the Exchanges are established at present. During the last six months of 1809, and the three first months of the present year, the Exchanges on Hamburgh and Amsterdam were depressed as low as from 16 to 20 per cent. below par ; and that on Paris still lower. The Exchanges with Portugal have corresponded with the others ; but they are complicated by some circumstances which shall be explained separately.

Your Committee find, that in the course of the month of March last, that is, from the 2nd of March to the 3rd April, the Exchanges with the three places above mentioned received a gradual improvement. The Exchange with Hamburgh rose gradually from 29.4 to 31 ; that with Amsterdam from 31.8 to 33.5 ; that with Paris from 19.16 to 21.11. Since the 3rd of April last to the present time, they have remained nearly stationary at those rates, the Exchange with Hamburgh, as stated in the tables printed for the use of the Merchants, appearing as much against this Country as £9 per cent. below par ; that with Amsterdam appearing to be more than £7 per cent. below par ; and that with Paris more than £14 per cent. below par.

So extraordinary a rise in the market price of Gold in this Country, coupled with so remarkable a depression of our Exchanges with the Continent, very early, in the judgment of Your Committee, pointed to something in the state of our own domestic currency as the cause of both appearances. But before they adopted that conclusion, which seemed agreeable to all former reasonings and experience, they thought it proper to enquire more particularly into the circumstances connected with each of those two facts ; and to hear, from persons of commercial practice, and detail, what explanations they had to offer of so unusual a state of things.

With this view, Your Committee called before them several Merchants of extensive dealings and intelligence, and desired to have their opinions with respect to the cause of the high price of Gold and the low rates of Exchange.

I

It will be found by the Evidence (*Minutes of Evidence*, pp. 41–45, 135, 136, 178, 179), that the high price of Gold is ascribed, by most of the Witnesses, entirely to an alleged scarcity of that article, arising out of an unusual demand for it upon the Continent of Europe. This unusual demand for Gold upon the Continent is described by some of them as being chiefly for the use of the French Armies, though increased also by that state of alarm, and failure of confidence, which leads to the practice of hoarding.

Your Committee are of opinion, that, in the sound and natural state of the British currency, the foundation of which is Gold, no increased demand for Gold from other parts of the world, however great, or from whatever causes arising, can have the effect of producing here, for a considerable period of time, a material rise in the market price of Gold. But before they proceed to explain the grounds of that general opinion, they wish to state some other reasons which alone would have led them to doubt whether, in point of fact, such a demand for Gold, as is alleged, has operated in the manner supposed.

If there were an unusual demand for Gold upon the Continent, such as could influence its market price in this country, it would of course influence also, and indeed in the first instance, its price in the Continental markets ; and it was to be expected that those who ascribed the high price here to a great demand abroad, would have been prepared to state that there was a corresponding high price abroad. Your Committee did not find that they grounded their inference upon any such information ; and so far as Your Committee have been enabled to ascertain, it does not appear that during the period when the price of Gold Bullion was rising here, as valued in our paper, there was any corresponding rise in the price of Gold Bullion in the market of the Continent, as valued in their respective currencies. *Mr. Whitmore*, indeed, the late Governor of the Bank, stated, (*Min.* pp. 178, 179), that in his opinion it was the high price abroad which had carried our Gold coin out of this Country; but he did not offer to Your Committee any proof of this high price. *Mr. Greffulhe*, a Continental Merchant (*Min.* p. 70), who appeared to be remarkably well informed in the details of trade, being asked by the Committee, If he could state whether any change had taken place in the price of Gold in any of the foreign markets within the last year? answered, " No very material change that I am aware of." Upon a subsequent day (*Min.* pp. 131, 132), having had time to refer to the actual prices, he again stated to the Committee, " I beg " leave to observe, that there has been no alteration of late " in the Mint price of Gold in foreign places, nor have the " market prices experienced an advance at all relative to the " rise that has taken place in England ; one of the papers " I have delivered shews the foreign prices reduced into " sterling money at the present low rates of Exchange, and " the excess above our market price may be considered as " about equal to the charges of conveyance." The paper he refers to will be found in the Appendix (*Appendix of Accounts ;* No. 56, 57, 58), and this statement made by Mr. Greffulhe throws great light upon this part of the subject ; as it shews, that the actual prices of Gold in the foreign markets are just so much lower than its market price here, as the difference of Exchange amounts to. Mr. Greffulhe's paper is confirmed by another (*Acc.* No. 59, *Min.* p. 116), which has been laid before Your Committee. *Mr. Abraham Goldsmid* has also stated to Your Committee, that, during that part of last year when the market price of Gold here rose so high, its price at Hamburgh did not fluctuate more than from 3 to 4 per cent.

Here Your Committee must observe, that both at Hamburgh and Amsterdam, where the measure of value is not Gold as in this Country, but Silver, an unusual demand for Gold would affect its money price, that is, its price in Silver ;

and that as it does not appear that there has been any
considerable rise in the price of Gold, as valued in Silver,
at those places in the last year, the inference is, that there
was not any considerable increase in the demand for Gold.
That permanent rise in the market price of Gold above
its Mint price, which appears by Mr. Greffulhe's paper to have
taken place for several years both at Hamburgh and Amsterdam, may in some degree be ascribed, as Your Committee
conceive, to an alteration which has taken place in the relative value of the two precious metals all over the world ;
concerning which, much curious and satisfactory Evidence
will be found in the Appendix, particularly in the documents
laid before Your Committee by Mr. Allen. (*Acc.* No. 21
to 33). From the same cause, a fall in the relative price
of Silver appears to have taken place in this Country for
some time before the increase of our paper currency began to operate. Silver having fallen in its relative value
to Gold throughout the world, Gold has appeared to rise
in price in those markets where Silver is the fixed measure,
and Silver has appeared to fall in those where Gold is the
fixed measure.

With respect to the alleged demand for Gold upon the
Continent for the supply of the French Armies, Your Committee must further observe, that, if the wants of the
military chest have been latterly much increased, the general
supply of Europe with Gold has been augmented by all
that quantity which this great commercial Country has
spared in consequence of the substitution of another medium
of circulation. And Your Committee cannot omit remarking,
that though the circumstances which might occasion such
an increased demand may recently have existed in greater
force than at former periods, yet in the former wars and
convulsions of the Continent, they must have existed in such
a degree as to produce some effect. *Sir Francis Baring*
has very justly referred (*Min.* p. 199) to the seven years'
war and to the American war, and remarks, that no
want of Bullion was then felt in this Country. And upon
referring for a course of years to the tables which are published for the use of the Merchants, such as Lloyd's Lists and

Wettenhall's Course of Exchange, Your Committee have
found that from the middle of the year 1773, when the
reformation of the Gold coin took place, till about the middle
of the year 1799, two years after the suspension of the cash
payments of the Bank, the market price of standard Gold
in bars remained steadily uniform at the price of £3 17s. 6d.
[being, with the small allowance for loss by detention at the
Mint, equal to the Mint price of £3 17s. 10½d.] with the
exception of one year, from May 1783 to May 1784, when it
was occasionally £3 18s. During the same period it is to be
noticed, the price of Portugal Gold coin was occasionally
as high as £4 2s. and Your Committee also observe, that it
was stated to the Lords' Committee in 1797 by Mr. Abraham Newland (*Report Comm. of Secresy*, p. 66), that the
Bank had been frequently obliged to buy Gold higher than
the Mint price, and upon one particular occasion gave as
much for a small quantity, which their agent procured from
Portugal, as £4 8s. But Your Committee find, that the
price of standard Gold in bars was never for any length
of time materially above the Mint price, during the whole
period of 24 years which elapsed from the reformation of
the Gold coin to the suspension of the cash payments of
the Bank. The two most remarkable periods prior to the
present, when the market price of Gold in this country
has exceeded our Mint price, were in the reign of King
William, when the Silver coin was very much worn below
its standard, and in the early part of His present Majesty's
reign, when the Gold coin was very much worn below its
standard. In both those periods, the excess of the market
price of Gold above its Mint price was found to be owing
to the bad state of the currency ; and in both instances, the
reformation of the currency effectually lowered the market
price of Gold to the level of the Mint price. During the
whole of the years 1796 and 1797, in which there was
such a scarcity of Gold, occasioned by the great demands of
the country Bankers in order to increase their deposits, the
market price of Gold never rose above the Mint price.

Your Committee have still further to remark upon this
point, that the Evidence laid before them has led them to

entertain much doubt of the alleged fact, that a scarcity
of Gold Bullion has been recently experienced in this country.
That Guineas have disappeared from the circulation, there
can be no question ; but that does not prove a scarcity
of Bullion, any more than the high price proves that scarcity.
If Gold is rendered dear by any other cause than scarcity,
those who cannot purchase it without paying the high price,
will be very apt to conclude that it is scarce. A very extensive home dealer who was examined, and who spoke very
much of the scarcity of Gold, acknowledged (*Min.* p. 35),
that he found no difficulty in getting any quantity he wanted,
if he was willing to pay the price for it. And it appears to
Your Committee, that, though in the course of the last
year there have been large exportations of Gold to the
Continent, there have been also very considerable importations of it into this Country from South America, chiefly through the West Indies. The changes which have
affected Spain and Portugal, combined with our maritime
and commercial advantages, would seem to have rendered
this country a channel through which the produce of the
mines of New Spain and the Brazils passes to the rest
of the world. In such a situation, the imports of Bullion
and Coin give us the opportunity of first supplying ourselves ; and must render this the last of the great markets
in which a scarcity of that article will be felt. This is
remarkably illustrated by the fact, that Portugal Gold
coin is now sent regularly from this Country to the
Cotton Settlements in the Brazils, Pernambuco, and
Maranham, while Dollars are remitted in considerable
quantities to this country from Rio Janeiro.

It is important also to observe, that the rise in the market
price of Silver in this country, which has nearly corresponded
to that of the market price of Gold, cannot in any degree be
ascribed to a scarcity of Silver. The importations of Silver
have of late years been unusually large, while the usual
drain for India and China has been stopped. (*Acc.* Nos. 9
& 10.)

For all these reasons, Your Committee would be inclined to think, that those who ascribe the high price of

Gold to an unusual demand for that article, and a consequent scarcity, assume facts as certain of which there is no evidence. But even if these assumptions were proved, —to ascribe the high price of Gold in this Country to its scarcity, seems to your Committee to involve a misconception, which they think it important to explain.

In this Country, Gold is itself the measure of all exchangeable value, the scale to which all money prices are referred. It is so, not only by the usage and commercial habits of the country, but likewise by operation of law, ever since the Act of the 14th of His present Majesty [finally rendered perpetual by an Act of the 39th year of the reign] disallowed a legal tender in Silver coin beyond the sum of £25. Gold being thus our measure of prices, a commodity is said to be dear or cheap according as more or less Gold is given in exchange for a given quantity of that commodity; but a given quantity of Gold itself will never be exchanged for a greater or a less quantity of Gold of the same standard fineness. At particular times it may be convenient, in exchange for Gold in a particular coin, to give more than an equal quantity of other Gold ; but this difference can never exceed a certain small limit ; and thus it has happened that the Bank, while liable to pay its notes in specie, has under particular emergencies been put to the necessity of purchasing Gold at a loss, in order to keep up or to repair its stock. But, generally speaking, the price of Gold, being itself measured and expressed in Gold, cannot be raised or lowered by an increased or diminished demand for it. An ounce of Gold will exchange for neither more nor less than an ounce of Gold of the same fineness, except so far as an allowance is to be made, if the one ounce is coined or otherwise manufactured and the other is not, for the expense of that coinage or manufacture. An ounce of standard Gold Bullion will not fetch more in our market than £3 17s. 10½d. unless £3 17s. 10½d. in our actual currency is equivalent to less than an ounce of Gold. An increase or diminution in the demand for Gold, or, what comes to the same thing, a diminution or increase in the general supply of Gold, will, no doubt, have a material effect upon the money prices of all other articles.

An increased demand for Gold, and a consequent scarcity
of that article, will make it more valuable in proportion
to all other articles ; the same quantity of Gold will purchase a greater quantity of any other article than it did
before : in other words, the real price of Gold, or the quantity
of commodities given in exchange for it, will rise, and the
money prices of all commodities will fall ; the money price
of Gold itself will remain unaltered, but the prices of all
other commodities will fall.   That this is not the present
state of things is abundantly manifest ; the prices of all
commodities have risen and Gold appears to have risen in
its price only in common with them.   If this common
effect is to be ascribed to one and the same cause, that
cause can only be found in the state of the currency of
this Country.

Your Committee think it proper to state still more specifically, what appear to them to be the principles which
govern the relative prices of Gold in Bullion and Gold
in Coin, as well as of Paper circulating in its place and
exchangeable for it.   They cannot introduce this subject
more properly, than by adverting to those simple principles and regulations, on which a coinage issuing from the
King's Mint is founded.

The object is, to secure to the people a standard of a
determinate value, by affixing a stamp, under the Royal
authority, to pieces of Gold, which are thus certified to
be of a given weight and fineness.   Gold in Bullion is
the standard to which the Legislature has intended that
the coin should be conformed and with which it should
be identified as much as possible.   And if that intention
of the Legislature were completely fulfilled, the coined Gold
would bear precisely the same price in exchange for all other
commodities, as it would have borne had it continued in
the shape of Bullion ; but it is subject to some small fluctuations.

First, there is some expense incurred in converting
Bullion into coin.   They who send Bullion to be coined,
and it is allowed to any one to send it, though they are
charged with no seignorage, incur a loss of interest by

the detention of their Gold in the Mint. This loss may hitherto have amounted to about £1 per cent. but it is to be presumed that the improvements of the system of the new Mint will cause the detention and consequent loss to be much smaller. This £1 per cent. has formed the limit, or nearly the limit, to the possible rise of the value of coin above that of Bullion ; for to suppose that coin could, through any cause, advance much above this limit, would be to assume that there was a high profit on a transaction, in which there is no risk, and everyone has an opportunity of engaging.

The two following circumstances conjoined, account for the depression of the Coin below the price of Bullion, and will show what must have been the limit to its extent before 1797, the period of the suspension of the Cash payments of the Bank of England. First, the Coin, after it had become current, was gradually diminished in weight by use, and therefore if melted would produce a less quantity of Bullion. The average diminution of weight of the present current Gold Coin below that of the same Coin when fresh from the Mint, appears by the Evidence (*Acc.* No. 20) to be nearly £1 per cent. This evil, in more ancient times, was occasionally very great. It was particularly felt in an early period of His present Majesty's reign, and led to the reformation of the Gold Coin in 1773. But it is now carefully guarded against, not only by the legal punishment of every wilful deterioration of the Gold Coin, but also by the regulation of the Statute, that Guineas, of which the full weight when fresh from the Mint is 5 dwts. $9\frac{33}{89}$ grains, shall not be a legal tender if worn below 5 dwts. 8 grs. ; the depreciation thus allowed being at the utmost 1·11 per cent. A still more material cause of depression is the difficulty under which the holders of Coin have been placed when they wished to convert it into Bullion. The Law of this Country forbids any other Gold Coin than that which has become light to be put into the melting-pot, and, with a very questionable policy, prohibits the exportation of our Gold Coin, and of any Gold, unless an oath is taken that it has not been produced from the Coin of this realm. It appears

by the Evidence, that the difference between the value of
Gold Bullion which may be sworn off for exportation, and
that of the Gold produced or supposed to be produced from
our own Coin, which by Law is convertible only to domestic
purposes, amounts at present to between 3s. and 4s. per
ounce.

The two circumstances which have now been mentioned
have unquestionably constituted, in the judgement of Your
Committee, the whole cause of that depression of the value
of the Gold Coin of this Country in exchange for commodities,
below the value of Bullion in exchange for commodities,
which has occasionally arisen or could arise at those times
when the Bank paid in specie, and Gold was consequently
obtainable in the quantity that was desired ; and the limit
fixed, by those two circumstances conjoined, to this excess
of the market price of Gold above the Mint price, was
therefore a limit of about 5½ per cent. The chief part of
this depression is to be ascribed to that ancient but doubtful
policy of this Country, which, by attempting to confine the
Coin within the Kingdom, has served, in the same manner
as permanent restrictions on the export of other articles, to
place it under a disadvantage, and to give to it a less value
in the market than the same article would have if subject
to no such prohibition.

The truth of these observations on the causes and limits
of the ordinary difference between the market and Mint price
of Gold, may be illustrated by a reference to the mode,
explained in the Evidence, of securing a fixed standard of
value for the great commercial payments of Hamburgh. The
payments in the ordinary transactions of life are made in a
currency composed of the coins of the several surrounding
States ; but Silver is the standard there resorted to in the
great commercial payments, as Gold is in England. No
difference analogous to that which occurs in this Country,
between the Mint and market price of Gold, can ever arise
at Hamburgh with regard to Silver, because provision is
made that none of the three causes above specified [the
expense of coinage, the depreciation by wear, or the obstruc-
tion to exportation], shall have any operation. The large

payments of Hamburgh are effected in Bank money, which consists of actual Silver of a given fineness, lodged in the Hamburgh Bank by the merchants of the place, who thereupon have a proportionate credit in the Bank books, which they transfer according to their occasions. The Silver being assayed and weighed with scarcely any loss of time, the first-mentioned cause of fluctuation in the relative value of the current medium compared with Bullion is avoided. Certain masses of it being then certified (without any stamp being affixed on the metal) to be of a given quantity and fineness, the value is transferred from individual to individual by the medium merely of the Bank books, and thus the wearing of the Coin being prevented, one cause of depreciation is removed. A free right is also given to withdraw, melt, and export it ; and thus the other and principal source of the occasional fall of the value of the current medium of payment, below that of the Bullion which it is intended to represent, is also effectually precluded.

In this manner, at Hamburgh, Silver is not only the measure of all exchangeable value, but it is rendered an invariable measure, except in so far as the relative value of Silver itself varies with the varying supply of that precious metal from the mines. In the same manner the usage, and at last the law, which made Gold Coin the usual and at last the only legal tender in large payments here, rendered that metal our measure of value : and from the period of the reformation of the Gold Coin down to the suspension of the Bank payments in specie in 1797, Gold Coin was not a very variable measure of value ; being subject only to that variation in the relative value of Gold Bullion which depends upon its supply from the mines, together with that limited variation which, as above described, might take place between the market and the Mint price of Gold Coin.

The highest amount of the depression of the Coin which can take place when the Bank pays in Gold, has just been stated to be about 5½ per cent. ; and accordingly it will be found, that in all the periods preceding 1797, the difference between what is called the Mint price and market price of Gold never exceeded that limit.

Since the suspension of Cash payments in 1797, however, it is certain, that, even if Gold is still our measure of value and standard of prices, it has been exposed to a new cause of variation, from the possible excess of that paper which is not convertible into Gold at will ; and the limit of this new variation is as indefinite as the excess to which that paper may be issued. It may indeed be doubted, whether, since the new system of Bank of England payments has been fully established, Gold has in truth continued to be our measure of value ; and whether we have any other standard of prices than that circulating medium, issued primarily by the Bank of England and in a secondary manner by the country Banks, the variations of which in relative value may be as indefinite as the possible excess of that circulating medium. But whether our present measure of value, and standard of prices, be this paper currency thus variable in its relative value, or continues still to be Gold, but Gold rendered more variable than it was before in consequence of being interchangeable for a paper currency which is not at will convertible into Gold, it is, in either case, most desirable for the public that our circulating medium should again be conformed, as speedily as circumstances will permit, to its real and legal standard, Gold Bullion.

If the Gold Coin of the Country were at any time to become very much worn and lessened in weight, or if it should suffer a debasement of its standard, it is evident that there would be a proportionable rise of the market price of Gold Bullion above its Mint price : for the Mint price is the sum in coin, which is equivalent in intrinsic value to a given quantity, an ounce for example, of the metal in Bullion ; and if the intrinsic value of that sum of Coin be lessened, it is equivalent to a less quantity of Bullion than before. The same rise of the market price of Gold above its Mint price will take place, if the local currency of this particular Country, being no longer convertible into Gold, should at any time be issued to excess. That excess cannot be exported to other countries, and, not being convertible into specie, it is not necessarily returned upon those who issued it ; it remains in the channel of circulation, and is gradually absorbed by increasing the prices of all commodities. An increase in the quantity of the local currency of a particular country, will raise prices in that country exactly in the same manner as an increase in the general supply of precious metals raises prices all over the world. By means of the increase of quantity, the value of a given portion of that circulating medium, in exchange for other commodities, is lowered ; in other words, the money prices of all other commodities are raised, and that of Bullion with the rest. In this manner, an excess of the local currency of a particular country will occasion a rise of the market price of Gold above its Mint price. It is no less evident, that, in the event of the prices of commodities being raised in one country by an augmentation of its circulating medium, while no similar augmentation in the circulating medium of a neighbouring country has led to a similar rise of prices, the currencies of those two countries will no longer continue to bear the same relative value to each other as before. The intrinsic value of a given portion of the one currency being lessened, while that of the other remains unaltered, the Exchange will be computed between those two countries to the disadvantage of the former.

In this manner, a general rise of all prices, a rise in the market price of Gold, and a fall of the Foreign Exchanges, will be the effect of an excessive quantity of circulating medium in a country which has adopted a currency not exportable to other countries, or not convertible at will into a Coin which is exportable.

II

Your Committee are thus led to the next head of their inquiry ; the present state of the Exchanges between this Country and the Continent. And here, as under the former head, Your Committee will first state the opinions which they have received from practical men, respecting the causes of the present state of the Exchange.

Mr. Greffulhe, a general merchant trading chiefly to the Continent, ascribed the fall of Exchange between London and Hamburgh, near 18 per cent. below par, in the year 1809 (*Min.* p. 63), "altogether to the commercial " situation ot this Country with the Continent ; to the " circumstance of the imports, and payments of Subsidies, " &c. having very much exceeded the exports." He stated, however, that he formed his judgment of the balance of trade in a great measure from the state of the Exchange itself, though it was corroborated by what fell under his observation. He insisted particularly on the large imports from the Baltic, and the wines and brandies brought from France, in return for which no merchandize had been exported from this Country. He observed, on the other hand, that the export of Colonial produce to the Continent had increased in the last year compared with former years ; and that during the last year there was an excess, to a considerable amount, of the exports of colonial produce and British manufactures to Holland above the imports from thence, but not nearly equal, he thought, to the excess of imports from other parts of the world, judging from the state of the Exchange as well as from what fell generally under his observation. He afterwards explained, (*Min.* p. 74), that it was not strictly the balance of trade, but the balance of payments, being unfavourable to this Country, which he assigned as the principal cause of the rate of Exchange ; observing also, that the balance of payments for the year may be against us, while the general exports exceed the imports. He gave it as his opinion (*Min.* p. 72), that the cause of the present state of Exchange was entirely commercial, with the addition of the foreign expenditure of Government ; and that an excess of imports above exports would account for the rates of Exchange continuing so high as 16 per cent. against this country, for a permanent period of time.

It will be found in the Evidence, that several other Witnesses agree in substance with *Mr. Greffulhe*, in this explanation of the unfavourable state of the Exchange ; particularly *Mr. Chambers* and *Mr. Coningham.*

Sir Francis Baring stated to the Committee (*Min.* p. 198), that he considered the two great circumstances which affect the Exchange in its present unfavourable state, to be the restrictions upon trade with the Continent, and the increased circulation of this Country in paper as productive of the scarcity of Bullion. And he instanced, as examples of a contrary state of things, the seven years' war, and the American war, in which there were the same remittances to make to the Continent for naval and military expenditure, yet no want of Bullion was ever felt.

The Committee likewise examined a very eminent Continental Merchant, whose evidence will be found to contain a variety of valuable information. That Gentleman states, (*Min.* pp. 78, 82, 96, 102,) that the Exchange cannot fall in any country in Europe at the present time, if computed in coin of a definitive value, or in something convertible into such coin, lower than the extent of the charge of transporting it, together with an adequate profit in proportion to the risk attending such transmission. He conceives (*Min.* p. 84) that such fall of our Exchange as has exceeded that extent in the last 15 months, must certainly be referred to the circumstance of our paper currency not being convertible into specie ; and that if that paper had been so convertible, and Guineas had been in general circulation, an unfavourable balance of trade could hardly have caused so great a fall in the Exchange as to the extent of 5 or 6 per cent. He explains his opinion upon the subject more specifically in the following Answers, which are extracted from different parts of his Evidence.

" To what causes do you ascribe the present unfavourable course of Exchange ?—The first great depreciation took place when the French got possession of the North of Germany, and passed severe penal decrees against a communication with this Country ; at the same time that a sequestration was laid upon all English goods and property, whilst the payments for English account were still to be made, and the reimbursements to be taken on this

Country; many more bills were in consequence to be sold
than could be taken by persons requiring to make payments
in England. The comunication by letters being also very
difficult and uncertain, middlemen were not to be found, as
in usual times, to purchase and send such bills to England for
returns ; whilst no suit at law could be instituted in the
Courts of Justice there against any person who chose to
resist payment of a returned bill, or to dispute the charges
of re-exchange. Whilst those causes depressed the Exchange, payments due to England only came round at
distant periods ; the Exchange once lowered by those
circumstances, and Bullion being withheld in England to
make up those occasional differences the operations between
this Country and the Continent have ,continued at a low rate,
as it is only matter of opinion what rate a pound sterling
is there to be valued at, not being able to obtain what it is
meant to represent." (*Min*. p. 88.)

" The Exchange against England fluctuating from 15
to 20 per cent. how much of that loss may be ascribed to
the effect of the measures taken by the enemy in the North
of Germany, and the interruption of intercourse which has
been the result, and how much to the effect of the Bank of
England paper not being convertible into cash, to which you
have ascribed a part of that depreciation ?—I ascribe the
whole of the depreciation to have taken place originally in
consequence of the measures of the enemy ; and its not having
recovered, to the circumstance of the paper of England not
being exchangeable for cash." (*Min*. p. 90.)

" Since the conduct of the enemy which you have described, what other causes have continued to operate on
the Continent to lower the course of Exchange ?—Very
considerable shipments from the Baltic, which were drawn
for and the bills negotiated immediately on the shipments
taking place, without consulting the interest of the Proprietors in this country much, by deferring such a nego-
tiation till a demand should take place for such bills :
The continued difficulty and uncertainty in carrying on
the correspondence between this Country and the Continent : The curtailed number of houses to be found on

the Continent willing to undertake such operations, either
by accepting bills for English account drawn from the
various parts where shipments take place, or by accepting
bills drawn from this Country, either against property
shipped, or on a speculative idea that the Exchange either
ought or is likely to rise : The length of time that is required before goods can be converted into cash, from the
circuitous routes they are obliged to take : The very large
sums of money paid to foreign Ship Owners, which in
some instances, such as on the article of Hemp, has amounted
to nearly its prime cost in Russia : The want of middlemen
who as formerly used to employ great capitals in Exchange
operations, who, from the increased difficulties and dangers
to which such operations are now subject, are at present
rarely to be met with, to make combined exchange operations, which tend to anticipate probable ultimate results."
(*Min.* p. 96.)

The preceding Answers, and the rest of this Gentleman's
Evidence, all involve this principle, expressed more or less
distinctly, that Bullion is the true regulator both of the
value of a local currency and of the rate of Foreign Exchanges ; and that the free convertibility of paper currency
into the precious metals, and the free exportation of those
metals, place a limit to the fall of Exchange, and not only
check the Exchanges from falling below that limit, but
recover them by restoring the balance.

Your Committee need not particularly point out in what
respects these opinions, received from persons of practical
detail, are vague and unsatisfactory, and in what respects
they are contradictory of one another ; considerable assistance however may be derived from the information which
the evidence of these persons affords, in explaining the true
causes of the present state of the Exchanges.

Your Committee conceive that there is no point of
trade, considered politically, which is better settled, than
the subject of Foreign Exchanges. THE PAR of Exchange between two Countries is that sum of the currency
of either of the two, which, in point of intrinsic value,
is precisely equal to a given sum of the currency of the

other ; that is, contains precisely an equal weight of Gold
or Silver of the same fineness. If 25 livres of France
contained precisely an equal quantity of pure Silver with
twenty shillings sterling, 25 would be said to be the Par
of Exchange between London and Paris. If one country uses Gold for its principal measure of value, and another
uses Silver, the par between those countries cannot be
estimated for any particular period, without taking into
account the relative value of Gold and Silver at that particular period ; and as the relative value of the two precious
metals is subject to fluctuation, the Par of Exchange between two such countries is not strictly a fixed point, but
fluctuates within certain limits. An illustration of this will
be found in the Evidence (*Min.* pp. 78, 79), in the calculation
of the Par between London and Hamburgh, which is estimated
to be 34/3½ Flemish shillings for a pound sterling. That *rate*
of exchange, which is produced at any particular period
by a balance of trade or payments between the two countries,
and by a consequent disproportion between the supply and
the demand of bills drawn by the one upon the other, is a
departure on one side or the other from the real and fixed
Par. But this real Par will be altered if any change takes
place in the currency of one of the two countries, whether
that change consists in the wear or debasement of a metallic
currency below its standard, or in the discredit of a forced
paper currency, or in the excess of a paper currency not
convertible into specie ; a fall having taken place in the
intrinsic value of a given portion of one currency, that
portion will no longer be equal to the same portion, as
before, of the other currency. But though the real Par
of the currencies is thus altered, the dealers, having little
or no occasion to refer to the par, continue to reckon their
course of Exchanges from the former denomination of the
par ; and in this state of things a distinction is necessary to
be made between the *real* and *computed* course of Exchange.
The computed course of Exchange, as expressed in the
tables used by the Merchants, will then include, not only
the real difference of exchange arising from the state of
trade, but likewise the difference between the original par

and the new par. Those two sums may happen to be
added together in the calculation or they may happen
to be set against each other. If the country, whose currency has been depreciated in comparison with the other,
has the balance of trade also against it, the computed
rate of exchange will appear to be still more unfavourable
than the real difference of exchange will be found to be ;
and so if that same country has the balance of trade in
its favour, the computed rate of exchange will appear to
be much less favourable than the real difference of exchange will be found to be. Before the new coinage of
our silver in King William's time, the Exchange between
England and Holland, computed in the usual manner
according to the standard of their respective mints, was
25 per cent. against England ; but the value of the current coin of England was more than 25 per cent. below
the standard value ; so that if that of Holland was at its
full standard, the real exchange was in fact in favour of
England. It may happen in the same manner, that the
two parts of the calculation may be both opposite and
equal, the real exchange in favour of the country by trade
being equal to the nominal exchange against it by the state
of its currency : in that case, the computed exchange
will be at par, while the real exchange is in fact in favour
of that country. Again the currencies of both the countries
which trade together may have undergone an alteration,
and that either in an equal degree, or unequally : in such
a case, the question of the real state of the exchange between
them becomes a little more complicated, but it is to be resolved exactly upon the same principle. Without going out
of the bounds of the present inquiry, this may be well
illustrated by the present state of the Exchange of
London with Portugal, as quoted in the tables for the
18th of May last. The exchange of London on Lisbon
appears to be 67½ ; 67½d. sterling for a mill ree is the old
established par of exchange between the two countries ;
and 67½ accordingly is still said to be the par. But by the
evidence of *Mr. Lyne*, it appears, (*Min.* p. 50) that, in
Portugal, all payments are now by law made one-half in hard

money, and one-half in Government paper ; and that this
paper is depreciated at a discount of 27 per cent. Upon
all payments made in Portugal, therefore, there is a discount
or loss of 13½ per cent. ; and the exchange at 67½, though
nominally at par, is in truth 13½ per cent. against this
Country. If the exchange were really at par, it would be
quoted at 56$\frac{65}{100}$, or apparently 13½ per cent. in favour of
London, as compared with the old par which was fixed
before the depreciation of the Portuguese medium of payments. Whether this 13½ per cent., which stands against
this Country by the present Exchange on Lisbon, is a real
difference of Exchange, occasioned by the course of trade
and by the remittances to Portugal on account of Government, or a nominal and apparent Exchange occasioned by
something in the state of our own currency, or is partly real
and partly nominal, may perhaps be determined by what
Your Committee have yet to state.

It appears to Your Committee to have been long settled
and understood as a principle, that the difference of Exchange resulting from the state of trade and payments
between two countries is limited by the expence of con-
veying and insuring the precious metals from one country to the other ; at least that it cannot for any considerable
length of time exceed that limit. The real difference of
Exchange, resulting from the state of trade and payments, never can fall lower than the amount of such
expense of carriage, including the Insurance. The truth
of this position is so plain, and it is so uniformly agreed
to by all the practical authorities, both commercial and
political, that Your Committee will assume it as indis-
putable.

It occurred however to Your Committee, that the amount
of that charge and premium of insurance might be increased
above what it has been in ordinary periods even of war,
by the peculiar circumstances which at present obstruct
the commercial intercourse between this Country and the
Continent of Europe ; and that as such an increase would
place so much lower than usual the limit to which our
Exchanges might fall, an explanation might thereby be

furnished of their present unusual fall. Your Committee
accordingly directed their enquiries to this point.

It was stated to Your Committee, by the Merchant
who has been already mentioned as being intimately acquainted with the trade between this Country and the
Continent (*Min.* pp. 83, 84), that the present expense of
transporting Gold from London to Hamburgh, indepen-
dent of the premium of Insurance, is from 1½ to 2 per
cent. ; that the risk is very variable from day to day, so
that there is no fixed premium, but he conceived the average
risk, for the fifteen months preceding the time when he
spoke, to have been about 4 per cent. : making the whole
cost of sending Gold from London to Hamburgh for those
fifteen months, at such average of the risk, from 5½ to 6 per
cent.—*Mr. Abraham Goldsmid* stated, that in the last five
or six months of the year 1809, the expense of sending Gold
to Holland varied exceedingly, from 4 to 7 per cent. for all
charges, covering the risk as well as the costs of transporta-
tion. By the Evidence which was taken before the Committees upon the Bank affairs in 1797, it appears that the
cost of sending specie from London to Hamburgh in that
time of war, including all charges as well as an average insurance, was estimated at a little more than 3½ per cent.
It is clear, therefore, that in consequence of the peculiar
circumstances of the present state of the war, and the increased
difficulties of intercourse with the Continent, the cost of
transporting the precious metals thither from this Country
has not only been rendered more fluctuating than it used
to be, but, upon the whole, is very considerably increased.
It would appear, however, that upon an average of the risk
for that period when it seems to have been highest, the last
half of the last year, the cost and insurance of transporting
Gold to Hamburgh or to Holland did not exceed 7 per cent.
It was of course greater at particular times, when the risk was
above that average. It is evident also that the risk, and
consequently the whole cost of transporting it to an inland
market, to Paris for example, would, upon an average, be
higher than that of carrying it to Amsterdam or Hamburgh.
It follows, that the limit to which the Exchanges, as

resulting from the state of trade, might fall and continue un-favourable for a considerable length of time, has, during the period in question, been a good deal lower than in former times of war ; but it appears also, that the ex-pense of remitting specie has not been increased so much, and that the limit, by which the depression of the Ex-changes is bounded, has not been lowered so much, as to afford an adequate explanation of a fall of the Ex-changes so great as from 16 to 20 per cent. below par. The increased cost of such remittance would explain, at those moments when the risk was greatest, a fall of some-thing more than 7 per cent. in the Exchange with Ham-burgh or Holland, and a fall still greater perhaps in the Exchange with Paris ; but the rest of the fall, which has actually taken place, remains to be explained in some other manner.

Your Committee are disposed to think, from the result of the whole evidence, contradictory as it is, that the circumstances of the trade of this Country, in the course of the last year, were such as to occasion a real fall of our Exchanges with the Continent to a certain extent, and perhaps at one period almost as low as the limit fixed by the expense of remitting Gold from hence to the re-spective markets. And Your Committee is inclined to this opinion, both by what is stated regarding the excess of imports from the Continent above the exports, though that is the part of the subject which is left most in doubt ; and also by what is stated respecting the mode in which the payments in our trade have been latterly effected, an advance being paid upon the imports from the Continent of Europe, and a long credit being given upon the ex-ports to other parts of the world.

Your Committee, observing how entirely the present depression of our Exchange with Europe is referred by many persons to a great excess of our imports above our exports, have called for an account of the actual value of those for the last five years ; and Mr. Irving, the Inspec-tor General of Customs, has accordingly furnished the most accurate Estimate of both that he has been enabled

to form. He has also endeavoured to forward the object of
the Committee, by calculating now much should be de-
ducted from the value of goods imported, on account of
articles in return for which nothing is exported. These
deductions consist of the produce of Fisheries, and of
imports from the East and West Indies, which are of the
nature of rents, profits, and capital remitted to Proprietors in this Country. The balance of trade in favour of
this Country, upon the face of the Account thus made up,
was

In 1805 about	£6,616,000
1806	£10,437,000
1807	£5,866,000
1808	£12,481,000
1809	£14,834,000

So far, therefore, as any inference is to be drawn from
the balance thus exhibited, the Exchanges during the
present year, in which many payments to this Country
on account of the very advantageous balances of the two
former years may be expected to take place, ought to be
peculiarly favourable.

Your Committee, however, place little confidence in
deductions made even from the improved document which
the industry and intelligence of the Inspector General has
enabled him to furnish. It is defective, as Mr. Irving
has himself stated, inasmuch as it supplies no account of the
sum drawn by Foreigners (which is at the present period
peculiarly large) on account of freight due to them for the
employment of their shipping, nor, on the other hand, of
the sum receivable from them (and forming an addition to
the value of our exported articles) on account of freight
arising from the employment of British shipping. It leaves
out of consideration all interest on capital in England
possessed by Foreigners, and on capital abroad belonging
to Inhabitants of Great Britain, as well as the pecuniary
transactions between the Governments of England and
Ireland. It takes no cognizance of contraband trade, and of
exported and imported Bullion, of which no account
is rendered at the Custom-house. It likewise omits a most

important article, the variations of which, if correctly stated, would probably be found to correspond in a great degree with the fluctuations of the apparently favourable balance ; namely the bills drawn on Government for our naval, military, and other expenses in Foreign parts. Your Committee had hoped to receive an account of these from the table of the House ; but there has been some difficulty and consequent delay in executing a material part of the Order made for them. It appears from " an Account, as far as it could be made out, of sums paid for Expenses Abroad in 1793, 4, 5, and 6," inserted in the Appendix of the Lords' Report on the occasion of the Bank Restriction Bill, that the sums so paid were,

In 1793	.	.	.	.	£2,785,252
4	.	.	.	.	£8,335,591
5	.	.	.	.	£11,040,236
6	.	.	.	.	£10,649,916

The following is an account of the official value of our Imports and Exports with the Continent of Europe alone, in each of the last five years :

	IMPORTS.	EXPORTS.	Balance in favour of Great Britain, reckoned in Official Value.
	£	£	£
1805	10,008,649	15,465,430	5,456,781
1806	8,197,256	13,216,386	5,019,130
1807	7,973,510	12,689,590	4,716,080
1808	4,210,671	11,280,490	7,069,819
1809	9,551,857	23,722,615	14,170,758

The balances with Europe alone in favour of Great Britain as exhibited in this imperfect statement, are not far from corresponding with the general and more accurate balances before given. The favourable balance of 1809 with Europe alone, if computed according to the actual value, would be much more considerable than the value of the same year, in the former general statement.

A favourable balance of trade on the face of the Account of Exports and Imports, presented annually to Parliament, is a very probable consequence of large drafts on Government for foreign expenditure ; an augmentation of exports, and a diminution of imports, being promoted and even enforced by the means of such drafts. For if the supply of bills drawn abroad, either by the Agents of Government, or by individuals, is disproportionate to the demand, the price of them in foreign money falls, until it is so low as to invite purchasers ; and the purchasers, who are generally Foreigners, not wishing to transfer their property permanently to England, have a reference to the terms on which the bills on England will purchase those British commodities which are in demand, either in their own country, or in intermediate places, with which the account may be adjusted. Thus, the price of the bills being regulated in some degree by that of British commodities, and continuing to fall till it becomes so low as to be likely to afford a profit on the purchase and exportation of these commodities, an actual exportation nearly proportionate to the amount of the bills drawn can scarcely fail to take place. It follows that there cannot be, for any long period, either a highly favourable or unfavourable balance of trade ; for the balance no sooner affects the price of bills, than the price of bills, by its re-action on the state of trade, promotes an equalization of commercial exports and imports. Your Committee have here considered Cash and Bullion as forming a part of the general mass of exported or imported articles, and as transferred according to the state both of the supply and the demand ; forming however, under certain circumstances, and especially in the case of great fluctuations in the general commerce, a peculiarly commodious remittance.

Your Committee have enlarged on the documents supplied by Mr. Irving, for the sake of throwing further light on the general question of the balance of trade and the Exchanges, and of dissipating some very prevalent errors which have a great practical influence on the subject now under consideration.

That the real Exchange against this Country with the
Continent cannot at any time have materially exceeded
the limit fixed by the cost at that time of transporting specie, Your Committee are convinced upon the principles
which have been already stated. That in point of fact
those Exchanges have not exceeded that limit, seems to
receive a very satisfactory illustration from one part of the
evidence of Mr. Greffulhe, who, of all the Merchants examined,
seemed most wedded to the opinion, that the state of the
balance of payments alone was sufficient to account for any
depression of the Exchanges, however great. From what
the Committee have already stated with respect to the par
of Exchange, it is manifest that the Exchange between
two countries is *at its real par*, when a given quantity of
Gold or Silver in the one country is convertible at the market
price into such an amount of the currency of that country,
as will purchase a bill of Exchange on the other country for
such an amount of the currency of that other country as will
there be convertible at the market price into an *equal* quantity of Gold or Silver of the same fineness. In the same
manner the real Exchange is in *favour* of a country having
money transactions with another, when a given quantity of
Gold or Silver in the former is convertible for such an
amount in the currency of that latter country, as will
there be convertible into a *greater* quantity of Gold or
Silver of the same fineness.

Upon these principles, Your Committee desired Mr.
Greffulhe to make certain calculations, which appear in
his Answers to the following Questions ; viz. :

" Supposing you had a pound weight troy of Gold of
the English standard at Paris, and that you wished by means
of that to procure a Bill of Exchange upon London, what
would be the amount of the Bill of Exchange which you
would procure in the present circumstances ?—I find
that a pound of Gold of the British standard at the present
market price of 105 francs, and the exchange at 20 livres,
would purchase a Bill of Exchange of £59 8s.

" At the present market price of Gold in London, how
much standard Gold can you purchase for £59 8s. ?

At the price of £4 12s. I find it will purchase 13 ounces of Gold, within a very small fraction.

" Then what is the difference per cent. in the quantity of Standard Gold which is equivalent to £59 8s. of our currency as at Paris and in London ?—About 8½ per cent.

" Suppose you have a pound weight troy of our standard Gold at Hamburgh, and that you wished to part with it for a Bill of Exchange upon London, what would be the amount of the Bill of Exchange, which, in the present circumstances, you would procure ?—At the Hamburgh price of 101, and the Exchange at 29, the amount of the Bill purchased on London would be £58 4s.

" What quantity of our standard Gold, at the present price of £4 12s. do you purchase for £58 4s. ?—About 12 ounces and 13 dwts.

" Then what is the difference per cent. between the quantity of standard Gold at Hamburgh and in London, which is equivalent to £58 4s. sterling ?—About 5½ per cent.

" Suppose you had a pound weight troy of our standard Gold at Amsterdam, and wished to part with it for a Bill of Exchange upon London, what would be the amount sterling of the Bill of Exchange which you would procure ?—At the Amsterdam price of 14½, Exchange 31·6, and Bank agio 1 per cent. the amount of the Bill on London would be £58 18s.

" At the present price of £4 12s. what quantity of our standard Gold do you purchase in London for £58 18s. sterling ?—12 oz. 16 dwts.

" How much is that per cent. ?—7 per cent." (*Min.* p. 133.)

Similar calculations, but made upon different assumed data, will be found in the evidence of Mr. Abraham Goldsmid. (*Min.* pp. 115, 116.) From these answers of Mr. Greffulhe, it appears, that when the computed Exchange with Hamburgh was 29, that is, from 16 to 17 per cent. below par, the real difference of Exchange, resulting from the state of trade and balance of payments was no more than 5½ per cent. against this Country ; that when the computed

Exchange with Amsterdam was 31·6, that is about 15 per cent. below par, the real Exchange was no more than 7 per cent. against this Country; that, when the computed Exchange with Paris was 20, that is 20 per cent. below par, the real Exchange was no more than 8½ per cent. against this Country. (*Min.* p. 133.) After making these allowances, therefore, for the effect of the balance of trade and payments upon our Exchanges with those places, there will still remain a fall of 11 per cent. in the Exchange with Hamburgh, of above 8 per cent. in the Exchange with Holland, and of 11½ per cent. in the Exchange with Paris, to be explained in some other manner.

If the same mode of calculation be applied to the more recent statements of the Exchange with the Continent, it will perhaps appear, that though the computed Exchange is at present against this Country, the real Exchange is in its favour.

From the foregoing reasonings relative to the state of the Exchanges, if they are considered apart, Your Committee find it difficult to resist an inference, that a portion at least of the great fall which the Exchanges lately suffered must have resulted not from the state of trade, but from a change in the relative value of our domestic currency. But when this deduction is joined with that which Your Committee have stated, respecting the change in the market price of Gold, that inference appears to be demonstrated.

III

In consequence of the opinion which Your Committee entertain, that, in the present artificial condition of the circulating medium of this Country, it is most important to watch the Foreign Exchanges and the market price of Gold, Your Committee were desirous to learn, whether the Directors of the Bank of England held the same opinion, and derived from it a practical rule for the control of their circulation ; and particularly whether, in the course of the last year, the great depression of the Exchanges, and the great rise in the price of Gold, had suggested to the Directors any suspicion of the currency of the Country being excessive.

Mr. WHITMORE, the late Governor of the Bank, stated to the Committee (*Min.* p. 111), that in regulating the general amount of the loans and discounts, he did " not " advert to the circumstance of the Exchanges ; it appearing " upon a reference to the amount of our notes in circulation, " and the course of Exchange, that they frequently have " no connexion." He afterwards said (*Min.* p. 112), " My opinion is, I do not know whether it is that of the " Bank, that the amount of our paper circulation has no " reference at all to the state of the Exchange." And on a subsequent day, Mr. Whitmore stated (*Min.* p. 174), that " the present unfavourable state of Exchange has no " influence upon the amount of their issues, the Bank having " acted precisely in the same way as they did before." He was likewise asked (*Min.* p. 110), Whether, in regulating the amount of their circulation, the Bank ever adverted to the difference between the market and Mint price of Gold ? and having desired to have time to consider that question, Mr. Whitmore, on a subsequent day, answered it in the following terms, which suggested these further questions :

" In taking into consideration the amount of your notes " out in circulation, and in limiting the extent of your " discounts to Merchants, do you advert to the difference, " when such exists, between the market and the Mint price " of Gold ?—We do advert to that, inasmuch as we do " not discount at any time for those persons who we know, " or have good reason to suppose, export the Gold.

" Do you not advert to it any further than by refusing " discounts to such persons ?—We do advert to it, inas- " much as whenever any Director thinks it bears upon " the question of our discounts, he presses to bring for- " ward the discussion.

" The market price of gold having, in the course of the " last year, risen as high as £4 10s. or £4 12s. has that " circumstance been taken into consideration by you, " so as to have had any effect in diminishing or enlarging " the amount of the outstanding demands ?—It has not

" been taken into consideration by me in that view."
(*Min.* p. 125.)

Mr. PEARSE, now Governor of the Bank, agreed with
Mr. Whitmore in this account of the practice of the Bank,
and expressed his full concurrence in the same opinion.

Mr. PEARSE.—" In considering this subject with reference
" to the manner in which Bank notes are issued, resulting
" from the applications made for discounts to supply the
" necessary want of Bank notes, by which their issue in
" amount is so controlled that it can never amount to an
" excess, I cannot see how the amount of Bank notes issued
" can operate upon the price of Bullion, or the state of
" the Exchanges, and therefore I am individually of opinion
" that the price of Bullion, or the state of the Exchanges,
" can never be a reason for lessening the amount of Bank
" notes to be issued, always understanding the control which
" I have already described.

" Is the Governor of the Bank of the same opinion
" which has now been expressed by the Deputy Governor ?

Mr. WHITMORE.—" I am so much of the same opin-
" ion, that I never think it necessary to advert to the
" price of Gold, or the state of the Exchange, on the days
" on which we make our advances.

" Do you advert to these two circumstances with a view
" to regulate the general amount of your advances ?—I do
" not advert to it with a view to our general advances,
" conceiving it not to bear upon the question." (*Min.* p. 126.)

And Mr. HARMAN, another Bank Director, expressed
his opinion in these terms :—" I must very materially alter
" my opinions, before I can suppose that the Exchanges
" will be influenced by any modifications of our paper
" currency." (*Min.* p. 221.)

These Gentlemen, as well as several of the Merchants
who appeared before the Committee, placed much reli-
ance upon an argument which they drew from the want
of correspondence in point of time, observable between
the amount of Bank of England Notes and the state of
the Hamburgh Exchange during several years ; and Mr.
Pearse presented a Paper on this subject, which is inserted

in the Appendix. (*Acc.* No. 49.) Your Committee would feel no distrust in the general principles which they have stated, if the discordance had been greater ; considering the variety of circumstances which have a temporary effect on exchange, and the uncertainty both of the time and the degree in which it may be influenced by any given quantity of paper. It may be added, that the numerical amount of Notes (supposing £1 and £2 Notes to be excluded from the statement) did not materially vary during the period of the comparison ; and that in the last year, when the general Exchanges with Europe have become much more unfavourable, the notes of the Bank of England, as well as those of the country Banks, have been very considerably increased. Your Committee however, on the whole, are not of opinion that a material depression of the Exchanges has been manifestly to be traced in its amount and degree to an augmentation of notes corresponding in point of time. They conceive, that the more minute and ordinary fluctuations of Exchange are generally referable to the course of our commerce ; that political events, operating upon the state of trade, may often have contributed as well to the rise as to the fall of the Exchange ; and in particular, that the first remarkable depression of it in the beginning of 1809, is to be ascribed, as has been stated in the evidence already quoted, to commercial events arising out of the occupation of the North of Germany by the troops of the French emperor. The evil has been, that the Exchange, when fallen, has not had the full means of recovery under the subsisting system. And if those occasional depressions, which arise from commercial causes, are not after a time successively corrected by the remedy which used to apply itself before the suspension of the cash payments of the Bank, the consequences may ultimately be exactly similar to those which a sudden and extravagant issue of paper would produce. The restoration of the Exchange used to be effected by the clandestine transmission of Guineas, which improved it for the moment, by serving as a remittance ; and unquestionably also in part, probably much more extensively, by the reduction of the

total quantity of the remaining circulating medium, to
which reduction the Bank were led to contribute by the
caution which every drain of Gold naturally excited.   Under
the present system, the former of these remedies must be
expected more and more to fail, the Guineas in circulation
being even now apparently so few as to form no important
remittance ; and the reduction of paper seems therefore the
chief, if not the sole corrective, to be resorted to.   It is
only after the Bank shall have for some time resumed its
cash payments, that both can again operate, as they did
on all former occasions prior to the restriction.

The Committee cannot refrain from expressing it to be
their opinion, after a very deliberate consideration of this
part of the subject, that it is a great practical error to
suppose that the Exchanges with Foreign Countries, and
the price of Bullion, are not liable to be affected by the
amount of a paper currency, which is issued without the
condition of payment in specie at the will of the holder.
That the Exchanges will be lowered, and the price of
Bullion raised, by an issue of such paper to excess, is not
only established as a principle by the most eminent authorities upon Commerce and Finance ; but its practical truth
has been illustrated by the history of almost every State
in modern times which has used a paper currency ; and
in all those countries, this principle has finally been resorted to by their Statesmen as the best criterion to judge
by, whether such currency was or was not excessive.

In the instances which are most familiar in the history
of Foreign Countries, the excess of paper has been usually
accompanied by another circumstance, which has no place
in our situation at present, a want of confidence in the
sufficiency of those funds upon which the paper had been
issued.   Where these two circumstances, excess and want
of confidence, are conjoined, they will co-operate and produce their effect much more rapidly than when it is the
result of the excess only of a paper of perfectly good credit ;
and in both cases, an effect of the same sort will be produced upon the Foreign Exchanges, and upon the price of
Bullion.   The most remarkable examples of the former

kind are to be found in the history of the paper currencies
of the British Colonies in North America, in the early part
of the last century, and in that of the assignats of the French
Republic : to which the Committee have been enabled to add
another, scarcely less remarkable (*Min.* p. 85), from the
money speculations of the Austrian Government in the
last campaign, which will be found in the Appendix. The
present state of the currency of Portugal affords, also, an
instance of the same kind.

Examples of the other sort, in which the depreciation
was produced by excess alone, may be gathered from the
experience of the United Kingdom at different times.

In Scotland, about the end of the seven years' war,
Banking was carried to a very great excess ; and by a
practice of inserting in their promissory notes an optional
clause of paying at sight, or in 6 months after sight with
interest, the convertibility of such notes into specie at the
will of the holder was in effect suspended. These notes
accordingly became depreciated in comparison with specie ;
and while this abuse lasted, the exchange between London and Dumfries, for example, was sometimes four per
cent. against Dumfries, while the exchange between London and Carlisle, which is not thirty miles distant from
Dumfries, was at par. The Edinburgh Banks, when any
of their paper was brought in to be exchanged for bills
on London, were accustomed to extend or contract the
date of the bills they gave, according to the state of the
Exchange ; diminishing in this manner the value of those
bills, nearly in the same degree in which the excessive
issue had caused their paper to be depreciated. This excess of paper was at last removed by granting bills on
London at a fixed date ; for the payment of which bills,
or, in other words, for the payment of which excess of
paper, it was necessary in the first instance to provide, by
placing large pecuniary funds in the hands of their London correspondents. In aid of such precautionary measures
on the part of the Edinburgh Banks, an act of parliament
prohibited the optional clauses, and suppressed ten and
five shilling notes. The Exchange between England and

Scotland was speedily restored to its natural rate; and
bills on London at a fixed date having ever since been
given in Exchange for the circulating notes of Scotland,
all material excess of Scottish paper above Bank of England has been prevented, and the Exchange has been
stationary. (*Wealth of Nations*, vol. 1. p. 492.—Report
of Committee upon Irish Exchange, 1804, Mr. Mansfield's
Evidence.)

The experience of the Bank of England itself, within
a very short period after its first establishment, furnishes
a very instructive illustration of all the foregoing principles and reasonings. In this instance, the effects of a
depreciation of the coin, by wear and clipping, were coupled
with the effect of an excessive issue of paper. The Directors
of the Bank of England did not at once attain a very accurate
knowledge of all the principles by which such an institution
must be conducted. They lent money not only by discount,
but upon real securities, mortgages, and even pledges of
commodities not perishable; at the same time the Bank
contributed most materially to the service of Government
for the support of the Army upon the Continent. By the
liberality of those loans to private individuals, as well as
by the large advances to Government, the quantity of the
notes of the Bank became excessive, their relative value was
depreciated, and they fell to a discount of 17 per cent. At
this time there appears to have been no failure of the public
confidence in the funds of the Bank; for its Stock sold for
110 per cent. though only 60 per cent. upon the subscriptions had been paid in. By the conjoint effect of this
depreciation of the paper of the Bank from excess, and of
the depreciation of the Silver coin from wear and clipping,
the price of Gold Bullion was so much raised, that Guineas
were as high as 30s.; all that had remained of good Silver
gradually disappeared from the circulation; and the Exchange with Holland, which had been before a little affected
by the remittances for the Army, sunk as low as 25 per cent.
under par, when the Bank notes were at a discount of 17 per
cent. Several expedients were tried, both by Parliament
and by the Bank, to force a better Silver coin into circula-

tion, and to reduce the price of Guineas, but without effect.
At length the true remedies were resorted to : first, by a
new coinage of Silver, which restored that part of the
currency to its standard value, though the scarcity of money
occasioned by calling in the old coin brought the Bank
into straights, and even for a time affected its credit ;
secondly, by taking out of the circulation the excess of
Bank Notes. This last operation appears to have been
effected very judiciously. Parliament consented to enlarge
the Capital Stock of the Bank, but annexed a condition,
directing that a certain proportion of the new subscriptions
should be made good in Bank Notes. In proportion to the
amount of Notes sunk in this manner, the value of those
which remained in circulation began presently to rise ; in a
short time the notes were at par, and the Foreign Exchanges
nearly so. These details are all very fully mentioned in
authentic tracts published at the time, and the case appears
to Your Committee to afford much instruction upon the
subject of their present Enquiry. (See a short Account
of the Bank, by Mr. Godfrey, one of the original Directors ;
and A short History of the last Parliament, 1699, by Dr.
Drake ; both in Lord Somers' Collection of Tracts.)

Your Committee must next refer to the confirmation
and sanction which all their reasonings receive from the
labours of the Committee of this House, which was appointed
in a former Parliament to examine into the causes of the
great depreciation of the Irish Exchange with England in
1804. Most of the mercantile persons who gave evidence
before that Committee, including two Directors of the Bank
of Ireland, were unwilling to admit that the fall of the Exchange was in any degree to be ascribed to an excess of the
paper currency arising out of the restriction of 1797 ; the
whole fall in that case, as in the present, was referred
to an unfavourable balance of trade or of payments ; and
it was also then affirmed, that " Notes issued only in
proportion to the demand, in exchange for good and convertible securities payable at specific periods, could not
tend to any excess in the circulation, or to any depreciation."
This doctrine, though more or less qualified by some of the

Witnesses, pervades most of the evidence given before that Committee, with the remarkable exception of Mr. Mansfield, whose knowledge of the effects of that over issue ot Scotch paper, which has just been mentioned, led him to deliver a more just opinion on the subject. Many of the Witnesses before the Committee, however unwilling to acknowledge the real nature of the evil, made important concessions, which necessarily involved them in inconsistency. They could not, as practical men, controvert the truth of the general position, that " the fluctuations of Exchange between two countries are generally limited by the price at which any given quantity of Bullion can be purchased in the circulating medium of the debtor country, and converted into the circulating medium of the creditor country, together with the insurances and charges of transporting it from the one to the other." It was at the same time admitted, that the expense of transporting Gold from England to Ireland, including insurance, was then under one per cent. ; that before the restriction, the fluctuations had never long and much exceeded this limit ; and moreover, that the exchange with Belfast, where Guineas freely circulated at the time of the investigation by that Committee, was then 1¼ in favour of Ireland, while the Exchange with Dublin, where only paper was in use, was £10 per cent. against that country. It also appeared from such imperfect documents as it was practicable to furnish, that the balance of trade was then favourable to Ireland. Still, however, it was contended that there was no depreciation of Irish paper, that there was a scarcity and consequent high price of Gold, and that the diminution of Irish paper would not rectify the Exchange. " The depreciation of Bank paper in Ireland (it was said by one of the Witnesses, a Director of the Bank of Ireland) is entirely a relative term with respect to the man who buys and sells in Dublin by that common medium ; to him it is not depreciated at all ; but to the purchaser of a Bill on London, to him in that relation, and under that circumstance, there is a depreciation of ten per cent." By thus avoiding all comparison with a view to the point

in issue, between the value of their own paper and that
of either the then circulating medium of this Country or
of Gold Bullion, or even of Gold coin then passing at a
premium in other parts of Ireland, they appear to have
retained a confident opinion, that no depreciation of Irish
paper had taken place.

It is further observable, that the value of a considerable
quantity of Dollars put into circulation by the Bank of
Ireland at this period, was raised to 5s. a Dollar, for the
professed purpose of rendering the new Silver coin con-
formable to the existing state of the Exchange ; a circumstance on which the Committee animadverted in their
Report, and which serves to shew that the Irish paper
currency could not stand a comparison with the standard
price of Silver, any more than with that of Gold Bullion,
with Gold in coin, or with the then paper currency of this
kingdom.

A fact was mentioned to that Committee on the evidence of Mr. Colville, a Director of the Bank of Ireland,
which, though it carried no conviction to his mind of the
tendency of a limitation of paper to lower Exchanges,
seems very decisive on this point. He stated, that in
1753 and 1754, the Dublin Exchange being remarkably
unfavourable, and the notes of the Dublin Bank being
suddenly withdrawn, the Exchange became singularly
favourable. The mercantile distress produced on that
occasion was great, through the suddenness of the operation ;
for it was effected, not by the gradual and prudential
measures of the several Banks, but through the violent
pressure which their unguarded issues had brought upon
them. The general result, however, is not the less observable.

With a view to the further elucidation of the subject
of the Irish Exchanges, which so lately attracted the attention of Parliament, it may be proper to remark, that
Ireland has no dealings in Exchange with foreign countries, except through London ; and that the payments
from Ireland to the Continent are consequently converted
into English currency, and then into the currency of the
countries to which Ireland is indebted. In the spring of

1804, the Exchange of England with the Continent was above par, and the Exchange of Ireland was in such a state that £118 10s. of the notes of the Bank of Ireland would purchase only £100 of those of the Bank of England. Therefore, if the notes of the Bank of Ireland were not depreciated, and it was so maintained, it followed that the notes of the Bank of England were at more than 18 per cent. premium above the standard coin of the two countries.

The principles laid down by the Committee of 1804 had probably some weight with the Directors of the Bank of Ireland ; for between the period of their Report (June 1804), and January 1806, the circulation of the notes of the Bank of Ireland was gradually (though with small occasional fluctuations), reduced from about three millions to £2,410,000, being a diminution of nearly ⅕th ; at the same time, all the currency which had been issued under the name of Silver Tokens was by law suppressed. The paper currency, both of the Bank of England, and of the English Country Banks, seems during the same period to have gradually increased. The combination of these two causes is likely to have had a material effect in restoring to par the Irish Exchange with England.

The Bank of Ireland has again gradually enlarged its issues to about £3,100,000, being somewhat higher than they stood in 1804, an increase probably not disproportionate to that which has occurred in England within the same period. Perhaps, however, it ought not to be assumed, that the diminution of issues of the Bank of Ireland between 1804 and 1806, would produce a coresponding reduction in the issues of private Banks in Ireland, exactly in the same manner in which a diminution of Bank of England paper produces that effect on the Country Banks in Great Britain ; because the Bank of Ireland does not possess the same exclusive power of supplying any part of that country with a paper currency, which the Bank of England enjoys in respect to the metropolis of the Empire. The Bank of England, by restricting the quantity of this necessary article in that important quarter, can more effectually secure the improvement of its value ; and every such improvement must necessarily lead, by a corresponding diminution in amount, to a similar augmentation of the value of Country Bank paper exchangeable for it. That the same diminution of the circulation of private Banks took place in Ireland is more than probable, for the private Banks in Ireland are accustomed to give Bank of Ireland paper for their own circulating notes when required to do so, and therefore could not but feel the effect of any new limitation of that paper for which their own was exchangeable.

It is due, however, in justice to the present Directors of the Bank of England, to remind the House, that the suspension of their cash payments, though it appears in some degree to have originated in a mistaken view taken by the Bank of the peculiar difficulties of that time, was not a measure sought for by the Bank, but imposed upon it by the Legislature for what were held to be urgent reasons of State policy and public expediency. And it ought not to be urged as matter of charge against the Directors, if in this novel situation in which their commercial Company was placed by the law, and intrusted with the regulation and control of the whole circulating medium of the Country, they were not fully aware of the principles by which so delicate a trust should be executed, but continued to conduct their business of discounts and advances according to their former routine.

It is important, at the same time, to observe, that under the former system, when the Bank was bound to answer its Notes in specie upon demand, the state of the Foreign Exchanges and the price of Gold did most materially influence its conduct in the issue of those Notes, though it was not the practice of the Directors systematically to watch either the one or the other. So long as Gold was demandable for their paper, they were speedily apprized of a depression of the Exchange, and a rise in the price of Gold, by a run upon them for that article. If at any time they incautiously exceeded the proper limit of their advances and issues, the paper was quickly brought back to them, by those who were tempted to profit by the market price of Gold or by the rate of Exchange. In this manner the evil soon cured itself. The Directors of the Bank having their apprehensions excited by the reduction of their stock of Gold, and being able to replace their loss only by reiterated purchases of Bullion at a very losing price, naturally contracted their issues of paper, and thus gave to the remaining paper, as well as to the Coin for which it was interchangeable, an increased value, while the clandestine exportation either of the coin, or the Gold produced from it, combined in improving the state of the Exchange, and in producing a corresponding diminution of the difference between the market price and Mint price of Gold, or of paper convertible into Gold.

Your Committee do not mean to represent that the manner, in which this effect resulted from the conduct which they have described, was distinctly perceived by the Bank Directors. The fact of limiting their paper as often as they experienced any great drain of Gold, is, however, unquestionable. Mr. Bosanquet stated, in his evidence before the Secret Committee of the House of Lords, in the year 1797, That in 1783, when the Bank experienced a drain of Cash which alarmed them, the Directors took a bold step, and refused to make the advances on the loan of that year. This, he said, answered the purpose of making a temporary suspension in the amount of the drain of their Specie. And all the three Directors who have been examined before Your Committee, represent some restriction of the Bank issues as having usually taken place at those periods antecedent to the suspension of the cash payments of the Bank, when they experienced any material run. A very urgent demand for Guineas, though arising not from the high price of Gold and the state of the Exchange, but from a fear of Invasion, occurred in 1793, and also in 1797, and in each of these periods the Bank restrained their discounts, and consequently also the amount of their Notes, very much below the demand of the Merchants. Your Committee question the policy of thus limiting the accommodation in a period of alarm, unaccompanied with an unfavourable Exchange and high price of Bullion ; but they consider the conduct of the Bank at the two last-mentioned periods, as affording illustration of their general disposition, antecedently to 1797, to contract their loans and their paper, when they found their Gold to be taken from them.

It was a necessary consequence of the suspension of cash payments, to exempt the Bank from that drain of Gold, which, in former times, was sure to result from an unfavourable Exchange and a high price of Bullion. And the Directors, released from all fears of such a drain, and no longer feeling any inconvenience from such a state of things, have not been prompted to restore the Exchanges and the price of Gold to their proper level by a reduction of their advances and issues. The Directors, in former times, did not perhaps perceive and acknowledge the principle more distinctly than those of the present day, but they felt the inconvenience, and obeyed its impulse ; which practically established a check and limitation to the issue of paper. In the present times, the inconvenience is not felt ; and the check, accordingly, is no longer in force. But Your Committee beg leave to report it to the House as their most clear opinion, that so long as the suspension of Cash Payments is permitted to subsist, the price of Gold Bullion and the general Course of Exchange with Foreign Countries, taken for any considerable period of time, form the best general criterion from which any inference can be drawn, as to the sufficiency or excess of paper currency in circulation ; and that the Bank of England cannot safely regulate the amount of its issues, without having reference to the criterion presented by these two circumstances. And upon a review of all the facts and reasonings which have already been stated, Your Committee are further of opinion, that, although the commercial state of this Country and the political state of the Continent, may have had some influence on the high price of Gold Bullion and the unfavourable Course of Exchange with Foreign Countries, this price, and this depreciation, are also to be ascribed to the want of a permanent check, and a sufficient limitation of the paper currency in this Country.

In connexion with the general subject of this part of their Report, the policy of the Bank of England respect-

ing the amount of their circulation, Your Committee
have now to call the attention of the House to another
topic, which was brought under their notice in the course
to their Enquiry, and which in their judgment demands
fhe most serious consideration. The Bank Directors, as
well as some of the Merchants who have been examined,
shewed a great anxiety to state to Your Committee a
doctrine, of the truth of which they professed themselves
to be most thoroughly convinced, that there can be no
possible excess in the issue of Bank of England paper,
so long as the advances in which it is issued are made
upon the principles which at present guide the conduct
of the Directors, that is, so long as the discount of mercantile Bills is confined to paper of undoubted solidity,
arising out of real commercial transactions, and payable
at short and fixed periods. That the Discounts should
be made only upon Bills growing out of real commercial
transactions, and falling due in a fixed and short period,
are sound and well-established principles. But that,
while the Bank is restrained from paying in specie, there
need be no other limit to the issue of their paper than
what is fixed by such rules of discount, and that during
the suspension of Cash payments the discount of good
Bills falling due at short periods cannot lead to any excess in the amount of Bank paper in circulation, appears
to Your Committee to be a doctrine wholly erroneous
in principle, and pregnant with dangerous consequences
in practice.

But before Your Committee proceed to make such
observations upon this theory as it appears to them to
deserve, they think it right to shew from the Evidence,
to what extent it is entertained by some of those individuals who have been at the head of the affairs of the Bank.
The opinions held by those individuals are likely to have an
important practical influence; and appeared to Your Committee, moreover, the best evidence of what has constituted
the actual policy of that establishment in its corporate
capacity.

Mr. Whitmore, the late Governor of the Bank, ex-

pressly states (*Min.* p. 91), "The Bank never force a
"Note in circulation, and there will not remain a Note
"in circulation more than the immediate wants of the
"public require; for no Banker, I presume, will keep
"a larger stock of Bank Notes by him than his imme-
"diate payments require, as he can at all times procure
"them." The reason here assigned is more particularly
explained by *Mr. Whitmore*, when he says (*Min.* p. 127),
"The Bank Notes would revert to us if there was a re-
"dundancy in circulation, as no one would pay interest
"for a Bank Note that he did not want to make use of."
Mr. Whitmore further states (*Min.* p. 127), "The criterion
"by which I judge of the exact proportion to be maintained
"between the occasions of the Public, and the issues of the
"Bank, is by avoiding as much as possible to discount what
"does not appear to be legitimate mercantile paper." And
further, when asked, What measure the Court of Directors
has to judge by, whether the quantity of Bank Notes out
in circulation is at any time excessive ? *Mr. Whitmore* states
that their measure of the security [*scarcity ?*] or abundance
of Bank Notes is certainly by the greater or less application that is made to them for the discount of good paper.

Mr. Pearse, late Deputy Governor, and now Governor of the Bank, stated very distinctly his concurrence
in opinion with *Mr. Whitmore* upon this particular point.
(*Min.* p. 126.) He referred "to the manner in which
"Bank Notes are issued, resulting from the applications
"made for discounts to supply the necessary want of Bank
"Notes, by which their issue in amount is so controlled
"that it can never amount to an excess." He considers
"the amount of the Bank Notes in circulation as being
"controlled by the occasions of the public, for internal
"purposes, and (*Min.* p. 157) that "from the manner in
"which the issue of Bank Notes is controlled, the public
"will never call for more than is absolutely necessary for
"their wants.

Another Director of the Bank, *Mr. Harman*, being
asked (*Min.* p. 220), If he thought that the sum total
of discounts applied for, even though the accommodation

afforded should be on the security of good bills to safe persons, might be such as to produce some excess in the quantity of the Bank issues if fully complied with ; he answered, " I think if we discount only for solid persons, " and such paper as is for real *bona fide* transactions, we " cannot materially err." And he afterwards states, that what he should consider as the test of a superabundance would be, " money being more plentiful in the market."

It is material to observe, that both *Mr. Whitmore* and *Mr. Pearse* state (*Min.* p. 19), that " the Bank does not " comply with the whole demand upon them for discounts, " and that they are never induced, by a view to their own " profit, to push their issues beyond what they deem con- " sistent with the public interest."

Another very important part of the Evidence of these Gentlemen upon this point, is contained in the following Extract (*Min.* p. 128) :

" Is it your opinion that the same security would exist " against any excess in the issues of the Bank, if the rate " of the discount were reduced from £5 to £4 per cent. ? " Answer.—" The security of an excess of issue would be, I " conceive, precisely the same." *Mr. Pearse.*—" I concur in that Answer."

" If it were reduced to £3 per cent. ? "—*Mr. Whitmore*, " I conceive there would be no difference, if our " practice remained the same as now, of not forcing a " note into circulation." *Mr. Pearse.*—" I concur in " that Answer."

Your Committee cannot help again calling the attention of the House to the view which this Evidence presents, of the consequences which have resulted from the peculiar situation in which the Bank of England was placed by the suspension of Cash payments. So long as the paper of the Bank was convertible into specie at the will of the holder, it was enough, both for the safety of the Bank and for the public interest in what regarded its circulating medium, that the Directors attended only to the character and quality of the Bills discounted, as real ones and payable at fixed and short periods. They could not much exceed the proper bounds in respect of the quantity and amount of Bills discounted, so as thereby to produce an excess of their paper in circulation, without quickly finding that the surplus returned upon themselves in demand for specie. The private interest of the Bank to guard themselves against a continued demand of that nature, was a sufficient protection for the public against any such excess of Bank paper, as would occasion a material fall in the relative value of the circulating medium. The restriction of cash payments, as has already been shown, having rendered the same preventive policy no longer necessary to the Bank, has removed that check upon its issues which was the public security against an excess. When the Bank Directors were no longer exposed to the inconvenience of a drain upon them for Gold, they naturally felt that they had no such inconvenience to guard against by a more restrained system of discounts and advances ; and it was very natural for them to pursue as before (but without that sort of guard and limitation which was now become unnecessary to their own security), the same liberal and prudent system of commercial advances from which the prosperity of their own establishment had resulted, as well as in a great degree the commercial prosperity of the whole Country. It was natural for the Bank Directors to believe, that nothing but benefit could accrue to the public at large, while they saw the growth of Bank profits go hand in hand with the accommodations granted to the Merchants. It was hardly to be expected of the Directors of the Bank, that they should be fully aware of the consequences that might result from their pursuing, after the suspension of cash payments, the same system which they had found a safe one before. To watch the operation of so new a law, and to provide against the injury which might result from it to the public interests, was the province, not so much of the Bank as of the Legislature : And, in the opinion of Your Committee, there is room to regret that this House has not taken earlier notice of all the consequences of that law.

By far the most important of those consequences is, that while the convertibility into specie no longer exists as a check to an over issue of paper, the Bank Directors have not perceived that the removal of that check rendered it possible that such an excess might be issued by the discount of perfectly good bills. So far from perceiving this, Your Committee have shown that they maintain the contrary doctrine with the utmost confidence, however it may be qualified occasionally by some of their expressions. That this doctrine is a very fallacious one, Your Committee cannot entertain a doubt. The fallacy, upon which it is founded, lies in not distinguishing between an advance of capital to Merchants, and an additional supply of currency to the general mass of circulating medium. If the advance of capital only is considered, as made to those who are ready to employ it in judicious and productive undertakings, it is evident there need be no other limit to the total amount of advances than what the means of the lender, and his prudence in the selection of borrowers, may impose. But, in the present situation of the Bank, intrusted as it is with the function of supplying the public with that paper currency which forms the basis of our circulation, and at the same time not subjected to the liability of converting the paper into specie, every advance which it makes of capital to the Merchants in the shape of discount, becomes an addition also to the mass of circulating medium. In the first instance, when the advance is made by notes paid in discount of a bill, it is undoubtedly so much capital, so much power of making purchases, placed in the hands of the Merchant who receives the notes ; and if those hands are safe, the operation is so far, and in this its first step, useful and productive to the public. But as soon as the portion of circulating medium, in which the advance was thus made, performs in the hands of him to whom it was advanced this its first operation as capital, as soon as the notes are exchanged by him for some other article which is capital, they fall into the channel of circulation as so much circulating medium, and form an addition to the mass of currency. The necessary effect of every such addition to the mass, is to diminish the relative value of any given portion of that mass in exchange for commodities. If the addition were made by notes convertible into specie, this diminution of the relative value of any given portion of the whole mass would speedily bring back upon the Bank, which issued the notes, as much as was excessive. But if by law they are not so convertible, of course this excess will not be brought back, but will remain in the channel of circulation, until paid in again to the Bank itself in discharge of the bills which were originally discounted. During the whole time they remain out, they perform all the functions of circulating medium ; and before they come to be paid in discharge of those bills, they have already been followed by a new issue of notes in a similar operation of discounting. Each successive advance repeats the same process. If the whole sum of discounts continues outstanding at a given amount, there will remain permanently out in circulation a corresponding amount of paper ; and if the amount of discounts is progressively increasing, the amount of paper, which remains out in circulation over and above what is otherwise wanted for the occasions of the Public, will progressively increase also, and the money prices of commodities will progressively rise. This progress may be as indefinite, as the range of speculation and adventure in a great commercial country.

It is necessary to observe, that the law, which in this Country limits the rate of interest, and of course the rate at which the Bank can legally discount, exposes the Bank to still more extensive demands for commercial discounts. While the rate of commercial profit is very considerably higher than five per cent. as it has lately been in many branches of our Foreign trade, there is in fact no limit to the demands which Merchants of perfectly good capital, and of the most prudent spirit of enterprise, may be tempted to make upon the Bank for accommodation and facilities by discount. Nor can any argument or illustration place in a more striking point of view the extent to which such of the Bank Directors, as were examined before the Committee, seem to have in theory embraced that doctrine upon which Your Committee have made these observations, as well as the practical consequences to which that doctrine may lead in periods of a high spirit of commercial adventure, than the opinion which Mr. Whitmore and Mr. Pearse have delivered ; that the same complete security to the public against any excess in the issues of the Bank would exist if the rate of discount were reduced from five to four, or even to three per cent. From the Evidence, however, of the late Governor and Deputy Governor of the Bank, it appears, that though they state the principle broadly, that there can be no excess of their circulation if issued according to their rules of discount, yet they disclaim the idea of acting up to it in its whole extent. Though they stated the applications for the discount of legitimate bills to be their sole criterion of abundance or scarcity, they gave Your Committee to understand, that they do not discount to the full extent of such applications. In other words, the Directors do not act up to the principle which they represent as one perfectly sound and safe, and must be considered, therefore, as possessing no distinct and certain rule to guide their discretion in controlling the amount of their circulation.

The suspension of Cash payments has had the effect of committing into the hands of the Directors of the Bank of England, to be exercised by their sole discretion, the important charge of supplying the Country with that quantity of circulating medium which is exactly proportioned to the wants and occasions of the Public. In the judgment of the Committee, that is a trust, which it is unreasonable to expect that the Directors of the Bank of England should ever be able to discharge. The most detailed knowledge of the actual trade of the Country, combined with the profound science in all the principles of Money and Circulation, would not enable any man or set of men to adjust, and keep always adjusted, the right proportion of circulating medium in a country to the wants of trade. When the currency consists entirely of the precious metals, or of paper convertible at will into the precious metals, the natural process of commerce, by establishing Exchanges among all the different countries of the world, adjusts, in every particular country, the proportion of circulating medium to its actual occasions, according to that supply of the precious metals which the mines furnish to the general market of the world. The proportion, which is thus adjusted and maintained by the natural operation of commerce, cannot be adjusted by any human wisdom or skill. If the natural system of currency and circulation be abandoned, and a discretionary issue of paper money substituted in its stead, it is vain to think that any rules can be advised for the exact exercise of such a discretion ; though some cautions may be pointed out to check and control its consequences, such as are indicated by the effect of an excessive issue upon Exchanges and the price of Gold. The Directors of the Bank of England, in the judgment of Your Committee, have exercised the new and extraordinary discretion reposed in them since 1797, with an integrity and a regard to the public interest, according to their conceptions of it, and indeed a degree of forbearance in turning it less to the profit of the Bank than it would easily have admitted of, that merit the continuance of that confidence which the public has so long and so justly felt in the integrity with which its affairs are directed, as well as in the unshaken stability and ample funds of that great establishment. That their recent policy involves great practical errors, which it is of the utmost public importance to correct, Your Committee are fully convinced ; but those errors are less to be imputed to the Bank Directors, than to be stated as the effect of a new system, of which, however it originated, or was rendered necessary as a temporary expedient, it might have been well if Parliament had sooner taken into view all the consequences. When Your Committee consider that this discretionary power, of supplying the Kingdom with circulating medium, has been exercised under an opinion that the paper could not be issued to excess if advanced in discounts to Merchants in good bills payable at stated periods, and likewise under an opinion that neither the price of Bullion nor the course of Exchanges need be adverted to, as affording any indication with respect to the sufficiency or excess of such paper, Your Committee cannot hesitate to say, that these opinions of the Bank must be regarded as in a great measure the operative cause of the continuance of the present state of things.

IV

Your Committee will now proceed to state, from the information which has been laid before them, what appears to have been the progressive increase, and to be the present amount of the Paper circulation of this Country, consisting primarily of the Notes of the Bank of England not at present convertible into specie ; and, in a secondary manner, of the Notes of the Country Bankers which are convertible, at the option of the holder, into Bank of England Paper. After having stated the amount of Bank of England Paper, Your Committee will explain the reasons which induce them to think that the numerical amount of that Paper is not alone to be considered as decisive of the question as to its excess : and before stating the amount of Country Bank Paper, so far as that can be ascertained, Your Committee will explain their reasons for thinking that the amount of the Country Bank circulation is limited by the amount of that of the Bank of England.

1. It appears from the Accounts laid before the Committees upon the Bank Affairs in 1797, that for several years previous to the year 1796, the average amount of Bank Notes in circulation was between £10,000,000 and £11,000,000, hardly ever falling below £9,000,000 and not often exceeding to any great amount £11,000,000.

The following Abstract of the several Accounts referred to Your Committee, or ordered by Your Committee from the Bank, will shew the progressive increase of the Notes from the year 1798 to the end of the last year.

Average Amount of Bank of England Notes in circulation in each of the following years :

	Notes of £5 and upwards, including Bank Post Bills.	Notes under £5.	Total.
	£	£	£
1798	11,527,250	1,807,502	13,334,752
1799	12,408,522	1,653,805	14,062,327
1800	13,598,666	2,243,266	15,841,932
1801	13,454,367	2,715,182	16,169,594
1802	13,917,977	3,136,477	17,054,454
1803	12,983,477	3,864,045	16,847,522
1804	12,621,348	4,723,672	17,345,020
1805	12,697,352	4,544,580	17,241,932
1806	12,844,170	4,291,230	17,135,400
1807	13,221,988	4,183,013	17,405,001
1808	13,402,160	4,132,420	17,534,580
1809	14,133,615	4,868,275	19,001,890

Taking from the Accounts the last half of the year 1809, the average will be found higher than for the whole year, and amounts to £19,880,310.

The Accounts in the Appendix give very detailed Returns for the first four months of the present year, down to the 12th May, from which it will be found that the amount was then increasing, particularly in the smaller Notes. The whole amount of Bank Notes in circulation, exclusive of £939,990 of Bank Post Bills, will be found on the average of the two Returns for the 5th and 12th May last, to be £14,136,610 in Notes of £5 and upwards, and £6,173,380 in Notes under £5, making the sum of £20,309,990, and, including the Bank Post Bills, the sum of £21,249,980.

By far the most considerable part of this increase since 1798, it is to be observed, has been in the article of small notes, part of which must be considered as having been introduced to supply the place of the specie which was deficient at the period of the suspension of cash payments. It appears however that the first supply of small notes, which was thrown into circulation after that event, was very small in comparison of their present amount; a large augmentation of them appears to have taken place from the end of the year 1799 to that of the year 1802; and a very rapid increase has also taken place since the month of May in the last year to the present time; the augmentation of these small notes from 1st May 1809 to the 5th of May 1810, being from the sum of £4,509,470 to the sum of £6,161,020.

The notes of the Bank of England are principally issued in advances to Government for the public service, and in advances to the Merchants upon the discount of their bills.

Your Committee have had an Account laid before them, of Advances made by the Bank to Government on Land and Malt, Exchequer Bills, and other securities, in every year since the suspension of cash payments; from which, as compared with the Accounts laid before the Committees of 1797, and which were then carried back for 20 years, it will appear that the yearly advances of the Bank to Government have upon an average, since the suspension, been considerably lower in amount than the average amount of advances prior to that event; and the amount of those advances in the two last years, though greater in amount than those of some years immediately preceding, is less than it was for any of the six years preceding the restriction of cash payments.

With respect to the amount of commercial discounts, Your Committee did not think it proper to require from the Directors of the Bank a disclosure of their absolute amount, being a part of their private transactions as a commercial Company, of which, without urgent reason, it did not seem right to demand a disclosure. The late Governor and Deputy Governor, however, at the desire of Your Committee, furnished a comparative Scale, in progressive numbers, shewing the increase of the amount of their discounts from the year 1790 to 1809, both inclusive. They made a request, with which Your Committee have thought it proper to comply, that this document might not be made public; the Committee therefore have not placed it in the Appendix to the present Report, but have returned it to the Bank. Your Committee however have to state in general terms, that the amount of discounts has been progressively increasing since the year 1796 ; and that their amount in the last year (1809) bears a very high proportion to their largest amount in any year preceding 1797. Upon this particular subject, Your Committee are only anxious to remark, that the largest amount of mercantile discounts by the Bank, if it could be considered by itself, ought never, in their judgment, to be regarded as any other than a great public benefit ; and that it is only the excess of paper currency thereby issued, and kept out in circulation, which is to be considered as the evil.

But Your Committee must not omit to state one very important principle, That the mere numerical return of the amount of Bank notes out in circulation, cannot be considered as at all deciding the question, whether such paper is or is not excessive. It is necessary to have recourse to other tests. The same amount of paper may at one time be less than enough, and at another time more. The quantity of currency required will vary in some degree with the extent of trade ; and the increase of our trade, which has taken place since the suspension, must have occasioned some increase in the quantity of our currency. But the quantity of currency bears no fixed proportion to the quantity of commodities ; and any inferences proceeding upon such a supposition would be entirely erroneous. The effective currency of the Country depends upon the quickness of circulation, and the number of exchanges performed in a given time, as well as upon its numerical amount ; and all the circumstances, which have a tendency to quicken or to retard the rate of circulation, render the same amount of currency more or less adequate to the wants of trade. A much smaller amount is required in a high state of public credit than when alarms make individuals call in their advances, and provide against accidents by hoarding ; and in a period of commercial security and private confidence, than when mutual distrust discourages pecuniary arrangements for

any distant time. But, above all, the same amount of
currency will be more or less adequate in proportion to
the skill which the great money-dealers possess in manag-
ing and economising the use of the circulating medium.
Your Committee are of opinion, that the improvements
which have taken place of late years in this Country, and
particularly in the district of London, with regard to the
use and economy of money among Bankers, and in the mode
of adjusting commercial payments, must have had a much
greater effect than has hitherto been ascribed to them, in
rendering the same sum adequate to a much greater amount
of trade and payments than formerly. Some of those
improvements will be found detailed in the Evidence ; they
consist principally in the increased use of Bankers' drafts
in the common payments of London ; the contrivance of
bringing all such drafts daily to a common receptacle, where
they are balanced against each other ; the intermediate
agency of Bill-brokers ; and several other changes in the
practice of London Bankers, are to the same effect, of
rendering it unnecessary for them to keep so large a deposit
of money as formerly. Within the London district, it
would certainly appear, that a smaller sum of money is
required than formerly to perform the same number of
exchanges and amount of payments, if the rate of prices
had remained the same. It is material also to observe, that
both the policy of the Bank of England itself, and the
competition of the Country bank paper, have tended to
compress the paper of the Bank of England, more and more,
within London and the adjacent district. All these circumstances must have co-operated to render a smaller
augmentation of Bank of England paper necessary to supply
the demands of our increased trade than might otherwise
have been required ; and shew how impossible it is, from
the numerical amount alone of that paper, to pronounce
whether it is excessive or not : a more sure criterion must
be resorted to, and such a criterion, Your Committee have
already shown, is only to be found in the state of the Exchanges, and the price of Gold Bullion.

The particular circumstances of the two years which

are so remarkable in the recent history of our circulation, 1793 and 1797, throw great light upon the principle which Your Committee have last stated.

In the year 1793, the distress was occasioned by a failure of confidence in the country circulation, and a consequent pressure upon that of London. The Bank of England did not think it advisable to enlarge their issues to meet this increased demand, and their Notes, previously issued, circulating less freely in consequence of the alarm that prevailed, proved insufficient for the necessary payments. In this crisis, Parliament applied a remedy, very similar in its effect, to an enlargement of the advances and issues of the Bank ; a loan of Exchequer Bills was authorized to be made to as many mercantile persons, giving good security, as should apply for them ; and the confidence with this measure diffused, as well as the increased means which it afforded of obtaining Bank Notes through the sale of the Exchequer Bills, speedily relieved the distress both of London and of the country. Without offering an opinion upon the expediency of the particular mode in which this operation was effected, Your Committee think it an important illustration of the principle, that an enlarged accommodation is the true remedy for that occasional failure of confidence in the country districts, to which our system of paper credit is unavoidably exposed.

The circumstances which occurred in the beginning of the year 1797, were very similar to those of 1793 ;— an alarm of Invasion, a run upon the Country Banks for Gold, the failure of some of them, and a run upon the Bank of England, forming a crisis like that of 1793, for which, perhaps, an effectual remedy might have been provided, if the Bank of England had had courage to extend instead of restricting its accommodations and issue of Notes. Some few persons, it appears from the Report of the Secret Committee of the Lords, were of this opinion at the time ; and the late Governor and Deputy Governor of the Bank stated to Your Committee (*Min.* pp. 153, 154) that they, and many of the Directors, are now satisfied, from the experience of the year 1797, that

the diminution of their Notes in that emergency increased
the public distress : an opinion in the correctness of which
Your Committee entirely concur.

It appears to Your Committee, that the experience
of the Bank of England in the years 1793 and 1797, con-
trasted with the facts which have been stated in the present
Report, suggests a distinction most important to be kept
in view, between that demand upon the Bank for Gold
for the supply of the domestic channels of circulation,
sometimes a very great and sudden one, which is occasioned
by a temporary failure of confidence, and that drain upon
the Bank for Gold which grows out of an unfavourable
state of the Foreign Exchanges. The former, while the
Bank maintains its high credit, seems likely to be best
relieved by a judicious increase of accommodation to the
Country : the latter, so long as the Bank does not pay
in specie, ought to suggest to the Directors a question,
whether their issues may not be already too abundant.

Your Committee have much satisfaction in thinking,
that the Directors are perfectly aware that they may err
by a too scanty supply in a period of stagnant credit,
And Your Committee are clearly of opinion, that although
it ought to be the general policy of the Bank Directors
to diminish their paper in the event of the long continuance
of a high price of Bullion and a very unfavourable Exchange, yet it is essential to the commercial interests of
this Country, and to the general fulfilment of those mercantile engagements which a free issue of paper may have
occasioned, that the accustomed degree of accommodation
to the Merchants should not be suddenly and materially
reduced ; and that if any general and serious difficulty
or apprehension on this subject should arise, it may, in
the judgment of Your Committee, be counteracted without
danger, and with advantage to the public, by a liberality
in the issue of Bank of England paper proportioned to the
urgency of the particular occasion. Under such circumstances, it belongs to the Bank to take likewise into their
own consideration, how far it may be practicable, consis-
tently with a due regard to the immediate interests of the

public service, rather to reduce their paper by a gradual reduction of their advances to Government, than by too suddenly abridging the discounts to the Merchants.

2. Before Your Committee proceed to detail what they have collected with respect to the amount of Country Bank paper, they must observe, that so long as the Cash payments of the Bank are suspended, the whole paper of the Country Bankers is a superstructure raised upon the foundation of the paper of the Bank of England. The same check, which the convertibility into specie, under a better system, provides against the excess of any part of the paper circulation, is, during the present system, provided against an excess of Country Bank paper, by its convertibility into Bank of England paper. If an excess of paper be issued in a country district, while the London circulation does not exceed its due proportion, there will be a local rise of prices in that country district, but prices in London will remain as before. Those who have the country paper in their hands will prefer buying in London where things are cheaper, and will therefore return that country paper upon the Banker who issued it, and will demand from him Bank of England Notes or Bills upon London ; and thus, the excess of country paper being continually returned upon the issuers for Bank of England paper, the quantity of the latter necessarily and effectually limits the quantity of the former. This is illustrated by the Account which has been already given of the excess, and subsequent limitation, of the paper of the Scotch Banks, about the year 1763. If the Bank of England paper itself should at any time, during the suspension of Cash payments, be issued to excess, a corresponding excess may be issued of Country Bank paper which will not be checked ; the foundation being enlarged, the superstructure admits of a proportionate extension. And thus, under such a system, the excess of Bank of England paper will produce its effect upon prices not merely in the ratio of its own increase, but in a much higher proportion.

It has not been in the power of Your Committee to obtain such information as might enable them to state,

with anything like accuracy, the amount of Country
Bank paper in circulation. But they are led to infer
from all the Evidence they have been able to procure on
this subject, not only that a great number of new Country Banks has been established within these last two years,
but also that the amount of issues of those which are of
an older standing has in general been very considerably increased : whilst on the other hand, the high state of mercantile and public credit, the proportionate facility of converting at short notice all public and commercial securities
into Bank of England paper, joined to the preference
generally given within the limits of its own circulation to
the paper of a well established Country Bank over that of
the Bank of England, have probably not rendered it necessary for them to keep any large permanent deposits of
Bank of England Paper in their hands, And it seems reason-
able to believe, that the total amount of the unproductive
stock of all the Country Banks, consisting of specie and Bank
of England paper, is much less at this period, under a circulation vastly increased in extent, than it was before the
restriction of 1797. The temptation to establish Country Banks, and issue Promissory Notes, has therefore
greatly increased. Some conjecture as to the probable
total amount of those issues, or at least as to their recent
increase, may be formed, as Your Committee conceive,
from the amount of the duties paid for stamps on the
reissuable notes of Country Banks in Great Britain. The
total amount of these duties for the year ended on the
10th of October 1808, appears to have been £60,522 15s. 3d,
and for the year ended on the 10th of October 1809, £175,129
17s. 7d. It must, however, be observed, that on the 10th
of October 1808, these duties experienced an augmentation
somewhat exceeding one-third ; and that some regulations
were made, imposing limitations with respect to the re-
issue of all notes not exceeding two Pounds two Shillings,
the effect of which has been to produce a much more than
ordinary demand for stamps or notes of this denomination within the year 1809. Owing to this circumstance,
it appears impossible to ascertain what may have been

the real increase in the circulation of the notes, not exceeding two Pounds two Shillings, within the last year ; but with respect of the notes of a higher value, no alteration having been made in the Law as to their re-issue, the following Comparison affords the best statement that can be collected from the Documents before the Committee, of the addition made in the year 1809 to the number of those Notes.

Number of Country Bank Notes exceeding £2 2s. each stamped in the years ended the 10th of October 1808, and 10th of October 1809, respectively.

	1808.	1809.
	No.	No.
Exceeding £2 2s. and not exceeding £5 5s.	666,071	922,073
Exceeding £5 5s. and not exceeding £20 .	198,473	380,006
Exceeding £20 and not exceeding £30 .	—	2,425
Exceeding £30 and not exceeding £50 .	—	674
Exceeding £50 and not exceeding £100 .	—	2,611

Assuming that the notes in the two first of these classes were all issued for the lowest denomination to which the duties respectively attach, and such as are most commonly met with in the circulation of country paper, viz. Notes of £5 and £10 (although in the second class there is a considerable number of £20), and even omitting altogether from the comparison the Notes of the three last classes, the issue of which Your Committee understands is in fact confined to the chartered Banks of Scotland, the result would be, that, exclusive of any increase in the number of notes under £2 2s. the amount of Country Bank paper stamped in the year ended the 10th of October 1809, has exceeded that of the year ended on the 10th of October 1808, in the sum of £3,095,340. Your Committee can form no positive conjecture as to the amount of Country Bank paper cancelled and withdrawn from circulation in the course of the last year. But considering that it is the

interest and practice of the Country Bankers to use the
same notes as long as possible ; that, as the law now stands,
there is no limitation of time to the reissuing of those not
exceeding £2 2s. ; and that all above that amount are
reissuable for three years from the date of their first issuing ;
it appears difficult to suppose that the amount of notes
above £2 2s. cancelled in 1809, could be equal to the whole
amount stamped in 1808 : but even upon that supposition,
there would still be an increase for 1809 in the notes of £5
and £10 alone, to the amount above specified of £3,095,340,
to which must be added an increase within the same
period of Bank of England Notes to the amount of about
£1,500,000, making in the year 1809 an addition in the
whole of between four and five millions to the circulation
of Great Britain alone, deducting only the Gold which may
have been withdrawn in the course of that year from actual
circulation, which cannot have been very considerable, and
also making an allowance for some increase in the amount
of such country paper, as, though stamped, may not be in
actual circulation. This increase in the general paper
currency in last year, even after these deductions, would
probably be little short of the amount which in almost
any one year, since the discovery of America, has been
added to the circulating coin of the whole of Europe.   Although, as Your Committee has already had occasion
to observe, no certain conclusion can be drawn from the
numerical amount of paper in circulation, considered
abstractedly from all other circumstances, either as to
such paper being in excess, or still less as to the proportion of such excess, yet they must remark, that the fact of
any very great and rapid increase in that amount, when
coupled and attended with all the indications of a depreciated circulation, does afford the strongest confirmatory
evidence, that, from the want of some adequate check,
the issues of such paper have not been restrained within their
proper limits.

Your Committee cannot quit this part of the subject
without further observing, that the addition of between
four and five millions sterling to the paper circulation of

this Country, has doubtless been made at a very small expense to the parties issuing it, only about £100,000 having been paid thereupon in stamps to the Revenue, and probably for the reasons already stated, no corresponding deposits of Gold or Bank of England Notes being deemed by the Country Banks necessary to support their additional issues. These parties therefore, it may be fairly stated, have been enabled under the protection of the law, which virtually secures them against such demands, to create within the last year or fifteen months, at a very trifling expense, and in a manner almost free from all present risk to their respective credits as dealers in paper money, issues of that article to the amount of several millions, operating, in the first instance and in their hands, as capital for their own benefit, and, when used as such by them, falling into and in succession mixing itself with the mass of circulation of which the value in exchange for all other commodities is gradually lowered in proportion as that mass is augmented. If Your Committee could be of opinion that the wisdom of Parliament would not be directed to apply a proper remedy to a state of things so unnatural, and teeming, if not corrected in time, with ultimate consequences so prejudicial to the public welfare, they would not hesitate to declare an opinion, that some mode ought to be devised of enabling the State to participate much more largely in the profits accruing from the present system ; but as this is by no means the policy they wish to recommend, they will conclude their observations on this part of the subject, by observing, that in proportion as they most fully agree with Dr. Adam Smith and all the most able writers and Statesmen of this Country, in considering a paper circulation constantly convertible into specie, as one of the greatest practical improvements which can be made in the political and domestic economy of any State ; and in viewing the establishment of the Country Banks issuing such paper as a most valuable and essential branch of that improvement in this Kingdom ; in the same proportion is Your Committee anxious to revert, as speedily as possible, to the former practice and state of things in this respect :

convinced on the one hand, that anything like a permanent and systematic departure from that practice must ultimately lead to results, which, among other attendant calamities, would be destructive of the system itself; and on the other, that such an event would be the more to be deprecated, as it is only in a Country like this, where good faith, both public and private, is held so high, and where, under the happy union of liberty and law, property and the securities of every description by which it is represented, are equally protected against the encroachments of power and the violence of popular commotion, that the advantages of this system, unaccompanied with any of its dangers, can be permanently enjoyed, and carried to their fullest extent.

Upon a review of all the facts and reasonings which have been submitted to the consideration of Your Committee in the course of their Enquiry, they have formed an Opinion, which they submit to the House:—That there is at present an excess in the paper circulation of this Country, of which the most unequivocal symptom is the very high price of Bullion, and next to that, the low state of the Continental Exchanges; that this excess is to be ascribed to the want of a sufficient check and control in the issues of paper from the Bank of England; and originally, to the suspension of cash payments, which removed the natural and true control. For upon a general view of the subject, Your Committee are of opinion, that no safe, certain, and constantly adequate provision against an excess of paper currency, either occasional or permanent, can be found, except in the convertibility of all such paper into specie. Your Committee cannot, therefore, but see reason to regret, that the suspension of cash payments, which, in the most favourable light in which it can be viewed, was only a temporary measure, has been continued so long; and particularly, that by the manner in which the present continuing Act is framed, the character should have been given to it of a permanent war measure.

Your Committee conceive that it would be superfluous to point out, in detail, the disadvantages which must result to the Country, from any such general excess of currency as lowers its relative value. The effect of such an augmentation of prices upon all money transactions for time; the unavoidable injury suffered by annuitants, and by creditors of every description, both private and public; the unintended advantage gained by Government and all other debtors; are consequences too obvious to require proof, and too repugnant to justice to be left without remedy. By far the most important portion of this effect appears to Your Committee to be that which is communicated to the wages of common country labour, the rate of which, it is well known, adapts itself more slowly to the changes which happen in the value of money, than the price of any other species of labour or commodity. And it is enough for Your Committee to allude to some classes of the public servants, whose pay, if once raised in consequence of a depreciation of money, cannot so conveniently be reduced again to its former rate, even after money shall have recovered its value. The future progress of these inconveniences and evils, if not checked, must, at no great distance of time, work a practical conviction upon the minds of all those who may still doubt their existence; but even if their progressive increase were less probable than it appears to Your Committee, they cannot help expressing an opinion, that the integrity and honour of Parliament are concerned, not to authorize, longer than is required by imperious necessity, the continuance in this great commercial Country of a system of circulation, in which that natural check or control is absent which maintains the value of money, and, by the permanency of that common standard of value, secures the substantial justice and faith of monied contracts and obligations between man and man.

Your Committee moreover beg leave to advert to the

temptation to resort to a depreciation even of the value of the Gold coin by an alteration of the standard, to which Parliament itself might be subjected by a great and long continued excess of paper. This has been the resource of many Governments under such circumstances, and is the obvious and most easy remedy to the evil in question. But it is unnecessary to dwell on the breach of public faith and dereliction of a primary duty of Government which would manifestly be implied in preferring the reduction of the coin down to the standard of the paper, to the restoration of the paper to the legal standard of the coin.

Your Committee therefore, having very anxiously and deliberately considered this subject, report it to the House, as their Opinion, That the system of the circulating medium of this Country ought to be brought back, with as much speed as is compatible with a wise and necessary caution, to the original principle of Cash payments at the option of the holder of Bank paper.

Your Committee have understood that remedies, or palliatives, of a different nature, have been projected; such as, a compulsory limitation of the amount of Bank advances and discounts, during the continuance of the suspension; or, a compulsory limitation, during the same period, of the rate of Bank profits and dividends, by carrying the surplus of profits above that rate to the public account. But, in the judgment of Your Committee, such indirect schemes, for palliating the possible evils resulting from the suspension of cash payments, would prove wholly inadequate for that purpose, because the necessary proportion could never be adjusted, and, if once fixed, might aggravate very much the inconveniences of a temporary pressure; and even if their efficacy could be made to appear, they would be objectionable as a most hurtful and improper interference with the rights of commercial property.

According to the best judgment Your Committee has been enabled to form, no sufficient remedy for the present, or security for the future, can be pointed out, except the Repeal of the Law which suspends the Cash Payments of the Bank of England.

In effecting so important a change, Your Committee are of opinion that some difficulties must be encountered, and that there are some contingent dangers to the Bank, against which it ought most carefully and strongly to be guarded. But all those may be effectually provided for, by intrusting to the discretion of the Bank itself the charge of conducting and completing the operation, and by allowing to the Bank so ample a period of time for conducting it as will be more than sufficient to effect its completion. To the discretion, experience, and integrity of the Directors of the Bank, Your Committee believe that Parliament may safely intrust the charge of effecting that which Parliament may in its wisdom determine upon as necessary to be effected ; and that the Directors of that great institution, far from making themselves a party with those who have a temporary interest in spreading alarm, will take a much longer view of the permanent interests of the Bank, as indissolubly blended with those of the Public. The particular mode of gradually effecting the resumption of cash payments ought therefore, in the opinion of Your Committee, to be left in a great measure to the discretion of the Bank, and Parliament ought to do little more than to fix, definitively, the time at which cash payments are to become as before compulsory. The period allowed ought to be ample, in order that the Bank Directors may feel their way, and that, having a constant watch upon the varying circumstances that ought to guide them, and availing themselves only of favourable circumstances, they may tread back their steps slowly, and may preserve both the course of their own affairs as a Company, and that of public and commercial credit, not only safe but unembarrassed.

With this view, Your Committee would suggest, that the Restriction on Cash payments cannot safely be removed at an earlier period than two years from the present time ; but Your Committee are of opinion, that early provision ought to be made by Parliament for

terminating, by the end of that period, the operation of
the several Statutes which have imposed and continued
that restriction.

In suggesting this period of two years, Your Committee
have not overlooked the circumstance, that, as the law
stands at present, the Bank would be compelled to pay
in cash at the end of six months after the ratification of a
definitive Treaty of Peace; so that if Peace were to be
concluded within that period, the recommendation of Your
Committee might seem to have the effect of postponing,
instead of accelerating, the resumption of payments. But
Your Committee are of opinion, that if Peace were immediately to be ratified, in the present state of our circulation
it would be most hazardous to compel the Bank to pay
cash in six months, and would be found wholly impractic-
able. Indeed, the restoration of Peace, by opening new
fields of commercial enterprise, would multiply instead of
abridging the demands upon the Bank for discount, and
would render it peculiarly distressing to the commercial
world if the Bank were suddenly and materially to restrict
their issues. Your Committee are therefore of opinion,
that even if Peace should intervene, two years should be
given to the Bank for resuming its payments; but that
even if the War should be prolonged, Cash payments should
be resumed by the end of that period.

Your Committee have not been indifferent to the consideration of the possible occurrence of political circumstances, which may be thought hereafter to furnish an argument in favour of some prolongation of the proposed period
of resuming cash payments, or even in favour of a new law
for their temporary restriction after the Bank shall have
opened. They are, however, far from anticipating a necessity, even in any case, of returning to the present system.
But if occasion for a new measure of restriction could be
supposed at any time to arise, it can in no degree be
grounded, as Your Committee think, on any state of the
Foreign Exchanges (which they trust that they have
abundantly shown the Bank itself to have the general
power of controlling), but on a political state of things

producing, or likely very soon to produce, an alarm at
home, leading to so indefinite a demand for cash for domestic
uses as it must be impossible for any Banking establishment
to provide against. A return to the ordinary system of
Banking is, on the very ground of the late extravagant
fall of the Exchanges and high price of Gold, peculiarly
requisite. That alone can effectually restore general
confidence in the value of the circulating medium of the
kingdom ; and the serious expectation of this event must
enforce a preparatory reduction of the quantity of paper,
and all other measures which accord with the true principles
of Banking. The anticipation of the time when the Bank
will be constrained to open, may also be expected to contribute to the improvement of the Exchanges ; whereas a
postponement of this era, so indefinite as that of six months
after the termination of the War, and especially in the event
of an Exchange continuing to fall (which more and more
would generally be perceived to arise from an excess of paper,
and a consequent depreciation of it), may lead, under an
unfavourable state of public affairs, to such a failure of
confidence (and especially among foreigners), in the determination of Parliament to enforce a return to the professed standard of the measure of payments, as may serve
to precipitate the further fall of the Exchanges, and lead
to consequences at once the most discreditable and
disastrous.

Although the details of the best mode of returning to
cash payments ought to be left to the discretion of the
Bank of England, as already stated, certain provisions
would be necessary, under the authority of Parliament,
both for the convenience of the Bank itself, and for the
security of the other Banking establishments in this Country
and in Ireland.

Your Committee conceive it may be convenient for
the Bank to be permitted to issue Notes under the value
of £5 for some little time after it had resumed payments in
specie.

It will be convenient also for the Chartered Banks of
Ireland and Scotland, and all the Country Banks, that

they should not be compelled to pay in specie until some time after the resumption of payments in Cash by the Bank of England ; but that they should continue for a short period upon their present footing, of being liable to pay their own notes on demand in Bank of England paper.

RESOLUTIONS

PROPOSED TO

THE HOUSE OF COMMONS,

ON THE REPORT OF THE COMMITTEE APPOINTED
TO INQUIRE INTO THE HIGH
PRICE OF BULLION,

BY

Francis Horner, Esquire,

AND

The Right Hon. N. Vansittart,

ALSO

THE SEVERAL DIVISIONS

WHICH TOOK PLACE IN CONSEQUENCE OF THE SAME.

TO WHICH IS ADDED,

A LIST OF PUBLICATIONS

OCCASIONED BY THE

𝕽eport of t𝔥e 𝕮ommittee.

———————

LONDON :

PRINTED FOR J. HATCHARD, BOOKSELLER TO HER
MAJESTY, OPPOSITE ALBANY,
PICCADILLY.

1811.

THE following Papers are printed in compliance with the wishes of several Gentlemen who are collecting the Pamphlets written on the Report of the Committee of the House of Commons.

PROCEEDINGS

HOUSE OF COMMONS.

ON Monday the 6th of May, 1811, Francis Horner, esq. Chairman of the Bullion Committee, moved the following Resolutions, in a Committee of the whole House.

1. THAT the only Money which can be iegally tendered in Great Britain, for any sum above twelve pence in the whole, is made either of Gold or Silver; and that the weight, standard, and denomination, at which any such Money is authorized to pass current, is fixed, under his Majesty's prerogative, according to law.

2. THAT since the 43d year of the reign of Queen *Elizabeth*, the Indentures of his Majesty's Mint have uniformly directed that all Silver used

for Coin should consist of 11$^{oz.}$ 2$^{dwts.}$ of fine Silver, and 18$^{dwts.}$ of Alloy in each pound Troy, and that the said pound Troy should be divided into 62 Shillings, or into other Coins in that proportion.

3. THAT since the 15th year of the reign of King *Charles* the Second, the Indentures of his Majesty's Mint have uniformly directed, that all Gold used for Coin, should consist of 11$^{oz.}$ of pure Gold and 1$^{oz.}$ of Alloy in each pound Troy; and that the said pound Troy should be divided and coined into 44 Guineas and one Half-Guinea, or into other Coins in that proportion.

4. THAT by a Proclamation of the 4th year of the reign of King *George* the First, it was ordered and directed, that Guineas and the several other Gold Coins therein named, should be current at the Rates and Values then set upon them ; viz. The Guinea at the rate of 21 Shillings, and other Gold Coins in the same proportion : thereby establishing, that the Gold and Silver Coins of the Realm should be a legal tender in all Money Payments, and a Standard Measure for ascertaining the value of all contracts for the payment of Money, in the relative proportion of 15 $\frac{2852}{13640}$ Pounds weight of Sterling Silver to one Pound of Sterling Gold.

5. THAT by a Statute of the 14th year of the reign of His present Majesty, subsequently re-

vived and made perpetual by a Statute of the 39th year of his reign, it is Enacted, That no Tender in payment of Money made in the Silver Coin of this Realm, of any sum exceeding the sum of 25*l.* at any one time, shall be reputed in law, or allowed to be legal tender, within Great Britain or Ireland, for more than according to its *value by weight*, after the rate of 5*s.* 2*d.* for each Ounce of Silver.

6. THAT by a Proclamation of the 16th year of the reign of His present Majesty, confirmed by several subsequent Proclamations, it was ordered and directed, that if the *weight* of any Guinea shall be less than 5$^{dwts.}$ 8$^{grs.}$ such Guinea shall cease to be a legal tender for the payment of any Money within Great Britain or Ireland; and so in the same proportion for any other Gold Coin.

7. THAT under these laws (which constitute the established policy of this Realm, in regard to Money,) no contract or undertaking for the payment of Money, stipulated to be paid in Pounds Sterling, or in good and lawful Money of Great Britain, can be legally satisfied and discharged, in Gold Coin, unless the Coin tendered shall weigh in the proportion of $\frac{20}{21}$ parts of 5$^{dwts.}$ 8$^{grs.}$ of Standard Gold for each Pound Sterling, specified in the said contract; nor in Silver Coin, for a sum exceeding 25*l.* unless such Coin shall weigh in the proportion

of $\frac{20}{63}$ of a Pound Troy of Standard Silver for each Pound Sterling specified in the contract.

8. THAT the Promissory Notes of the Bank of England are stipulations to pay, on demand, the Sum in Pounds Sterling, respectively specified in each of the said Notes.

9. THAT when it was enacted by the authority of Parliament, that the Payment of the Promissory Notes of the Bank of England in Cash should for a time be suspended, it was not the intention of Parliament that any alteration whatsoever should take place in the Value of such Promissory Notes.

10. THAT it appears, that the actual Value of the Promissory Notes of the Bank of England, (measuring such Value by weight of Standard Gold and Silver as aforesaid,) has been, for a considerable period of time, and still is, considerably less than what is established by the laws of the Realm to be the legal Tender in payment of any Money contract or stipulation.

11. THAT the Fall which has thus taken place in the Value of the Promissory Notes of the Bank of England, and in that of the Country Bank Paper, which is exchangeable for it, has been occa-

sioned by too abundant Issue of Paper Currency, both by the Bank of England, and by the Country Banks; and that this Excess has originated from the want of that Check and Control on the Issues of the Bank of England, which existed before the Suspension of Cash Payments.

12. THAT it appears, that the Exchanges with Foreign Parts have, for a considerable period of time, been unfavourable to this Country, in an extraordinary degree.

13. THAT, although the adverse circumstances of our Trade, together with the large amount of our Military Expenditure Abroad, may have contributed to render our Exchanges with the Continent of Europe unfavourable ; yet the extraordinary degree, in which the Exchanges have been depressed for so long a period, has been in a great measure occasioned by the depreciation, which has taken place in the relative Value of the Currency of this Country as compared with the Money of Foreign Countries.

14. THAT during the continuance of the suspension of Cash Payments, it is the duty of the Directors of the Bank of England to advert to the state of the Foreign Exchanges, as well as to the price of Bullion, with a view to regulate the amount of their Issues.

15. THAT the only certain and adequate security to be provided, against an Excess of Paper Currency, and for maintaining the relative Value of the Circulating Medium of the Realm, is the legal Convertibility, upon demand, of all Paper Currency into lawful Coin of the Realm.

16. THAT in order to revert gradually to this Security, and to enforce meanwhile a due Limitation of the Paper of the Bank of England as well as of all the other Bank Paper of the Country, it is expedient to amend the Act which suspends the Cash Payments of the Bank, by altering the time, till which the Suspension shall continue, from Six Months after the Ratification of a Definitive Treaty of Peace, to that of Two Years from the present Time.

These Resolutions were debated on the 6th, 7th, 8th, and 9th of May, when the Fifteen first Resolutions were negatived by a Majority of 150 to 75, and the last Resolution by a Majority of 181 to 47.

ON the 13th of May — the Right Honourable
N. Vansittart moved the following Resolutions in
the same Committee.

1. *Resolved*, That it is the opinion of this Committee, That the right of establishing and regulating the legal Money of this Kingdom hath at all
times been a Royal Prerogative, vested in the Sovereigns thereof, who have from time to time exercised the same as they have seen fit, in changing
such legal Money, or altering and varying the
value, and enforcing or restraining the circulation
thereof, by Proclamation, or in concurrence with
the Estates of the Realm, by Act of Parliament:
and that such legal Money cannot lawfully be de-
faced, melted down, or exported.

2. *Resolved*, That it is the opinion of this Committee, That the Promissory Notes of the Governor
and Company of the Bank of *England* are engagements to pay certain sums of Money, in the legal
coin of this Kingdom ; and that, for more than a
century past, the said Governor and Company were
at all times ready to discharge such Promissory Notes
in legal Coin of the Realm, until restrained from so
doing on the 25th of February 1797, by an Order
of Council, confirmed by Act of Parliament.

3. *Resolved*, That it is the opinion of this Committee, That the Promissory Notes of the said Com-

pany have hitherto been, and arc at this time, held in public estimation to be equivalent to the legal Coin of the Realm, and generally accepted as such in all peeuniary transactions to which such Coin is lawfully applicable.

4. *Resolved,* That it is the opinion of this Committee, That at various periods, as well before as since the said Restriction, the Exchanges between *Great Britain* and several other Countries have been unfavourable to *Great Britain:* and that during such periods, the prices of Gold and Silver Bullion, especially of such Gold Bullion as could be legally exported, have frequently risen above the Mint price ; and the coinage of Money at the Mint has been either wholly suspended or greatly diminished in amount : and that such circumstances have usually occurred when expensive Naval and Military operations have been carried on abroad, and in times of public danger or alarm, or when large importations of gtain from foreign parts have taken place.

5. *Resolvcd,* That it is the opinion of this Committee, That such unfavourable Exchanges, and rise in the price ef Bullion, occurred to a greater or less degree, during the wars carried on by King *William* the Third and Queen *Anne,* and also during part of the Seven Years War, and of the *American* War, and during the War and Scarcity of Grain in 1795 and 1796, when the difficulty of procuring

Cash or Bullion increased to such a degree, that on the 25th of February, 1797, the Bank of *England* was restrained from making payments in Cash by an Order of Council, confirmed and continued to the present time by divers Acts of Parliament; and the Exchanges became still more unfavourable, and the price of Bullion higher, during the scarcity which prevailed for two years previous to the Peace of *Amiens.*

6. *Resolved,* That it is the opinion of this Committee, That the unfavourable state of the Exchanges, and the high price of Bullion, do not, in any of the instances above referred to, appear to have been produced by the restriction upon Cash payments at the Bank of *England,* or by any excess in the issue of Bank Notes; inasmuch as all the said instances, except the last, occurred previously to any restriction on such Cash payments; and because, so far as appears by such information as has been procured, the price of Bullion has frequently been highest, and the Exchanges most unfavourable, at periods, when the issues of Bank Notes have been considerably diminished, and they have been afterwards restored to their ordinary rates, although those issues have been increased.

7. *Resolved,* That it is the opinion of this Committee, That during the period of nearly 78 years, ending with the 1st of January, 1796, and previous to the aforesaid restriction, of which period Accounts are before the House, the price of Standard Gold in bars has been at or under the Mint price 28 years and 5 months ; and above the said Mint price 48 years and 11 months ; and that the price of Foreign Gold Coin has been at or under 3*l*. 18*s. per* oz. 36 years and 7 months, and above the said price 39 years and 3 months ; and that during the remaining intervals no prices are stated.—And that, during the same period of 78 years, the price of Standard Silver appears to have been at or under the Mint price 3 years and 2 months only.

8. *Resolved,* That it is the opinion of this Committee, That during the latter part and for some time after the close of the *American* War, during the years 1781, 1782, and 1783, the exchange with *Hamburgh* fell from 34. 1. to 31. 5, being about 8 *per Cent.* ; and the price of Foreign Gold rose from 3*l*. 17*s*. 6*d*. tō 4*l*. 2*s*. 3*d. per* oz. and the price of Dollars from 5*s*. 4¼*d. per* oz. to 5*s*. 11¼*d*. and that the Bank Notes in circulation were reduced between March 1782 and September 1782, from 9,160,000*l*. to 5,995,000*l*. being a diminution of above one third, and continued (with occasional variations) at such reduced rate until December 1784 : and that the exchange with *Hamburgh* rose to 34. 6, and the price of Gold fell to 3*l*. 17*s*. 6*d*. and Dollars to 5*s*. 1½*d. per* oz. before the 25th of February,

1787, the amount of Bank Notes being then increased to 8,688,000*l.*

9. *Resolved,* That it is the opinion of this Committee, That the Amount of Bank Notes in February, 1787, was 8,688,000*l.* and in February 1791, 11,699,000*l.* ; and that during the same period, the sum of 10,704,000*l.* was coined in Gold ; and that the Exchange with *Hamburgh* rose about 3 *per cent.*

10. *Resolved,* That it is the opinion of this Committee, That the average amount of Bank Notes in the year 1795 was about 11,497,000*l.* and on the 25th of February, 1797, was reduced to 8,640,000*l.* during which time the exchange with *Hamburgh* fell from 36 to 35, being about 3 *per cent.* ; and the said amount was increased to 11,855,000*l.* exclusive of 1,542,000*l.* in Notes of 1*l.* and 2*l.* each, on the 1st of February, 1798, during which time the Exchange rose to 38. 2, being about 9 *per cent.*

11. *Resolved,* That it is the opinion of this Committee, That the average price of Wheat *per* quarter in *England,* in the year 1798, was 50*s.* 3*d.* ; in 1799, 67*s.* 5*d.* ; in 1800, 113*s.* 7*d.* ; in 1801, 118*s.* 3*d.* ; and in 1802, 67*s.* 5*d.* : The amount of Bank Notes of 5*l.* and upwards, was—

£.		£.	£.			£.
in 1798, about 10,920,400,	and under 5,	1,786,000,			12,706,400
in 1799 . 12,048,790	.	1,626,110,	making	13,674,906
in 1800 . 13,421,920	.	1,831,320,	together	15,253,740
in 1801 . 13,454,370	.	2,715,180,		16,169,55 0
in 1802 . 13,917,980	.	3,136,470,		17,054,450

That the Exchange with *Hamburgh* was, in January 1798, 38. 2; January, 1799, 37. 7; January, 1800, 32. ; January, 1801, 29. 8; being in the whole a fall of above 22 *per cent.*; in January, 1802, 32. 2. ; and December, 1802, 34. ; being in the whole a rise of about 13 *per cent.*

12. *Resolved,* That it is the opinion of this Committee, That, during all the periods above referred to, previous to the commencement of the war with *France* in 1793, the principal States of *Europe* preserved their independence, and the trade and correspondence thereof were carried on conformably to the accustomed law of nations ; and that although, from the time of the invasion of *Holland* by the *French* in 1795, the trade of *Great Britain* with the Continent was in part circumscribed and interrupted, it was carried on freely with several of the most considerable ports, and commercial correspondence was maintained at all times previous to the Summer of 1807.

13. *Resolved,* That it is the opinion of this Committee, That, since the month of November 1806, and especially since the Summer of 1807, a system

of exclusion has been established against the *British* trade on the Continent of *Europe,* under the influence and terror of the *French* power, and enforced with a degree of violence and rigour never before attempted ; whereby all trade and correspondence between *Great Britain* and the Continent of *Europe* has (with some occasional exceptions, chiefly in *Sweden,* and in certain parts of *Spain* and *Portugal)* been hazardous, precarious, and expensive, the trade being loaded with excessive freights to foreign shipping, and other unusual charges : and that the trade of *Great Britain* with the United States of *America* has also been uncertain and interrupted ; and that, in addition to these circumstances, which have greatly affected the course of payments between this Country and other Nations, the Naval and Military Expenditure of the United Kingdom in foreign parts has, for three years past, been very great; and the price of Grain, owing to a deficiency in the crops, higher than at any time, whereof the accounts appear before Parliament, except during the scarcity of 1800 and 1801 ; and that large quantities thereof have been imported.

14. *Resolved,* That it is the opinion of this Committee, That the amount of Currency necessary for carrying on the transactions of the Country must bear a proportion to the extent of its Trade and its public Revenue and Expenditure; and that the annual

amount of the Exports and Imports of *Great Britain*, on an average of three years, ending 5th January, 1797, was 48,732,651*l*. official value; the average amount of Revenue paid into the Exchequer, including Monies raised by Lottery, 18,759,165*l*. ; and of Loans, 18,409,842*l*. making together 37,169,007*l*. ; and the average amount of the Total Expenditure of *Great Britain*, 42,855,111*l*. ; and that the average amount of Bank Notes in circulation (all of which were for 5*l*. or upwards) was about 10,782,780*l*. ; and that 57,274,617*l*. had been coined in Gold during His Majesty's reign, of which a large sum was then in circulation.

That the annual amount of the Exports and Imports of *Great Britain*, on an average of three years, ending 5th January, 1811, supposing the Imports from the *East Indies* and *China* to have been equal to their amount in the preceding year, was 77,971,318*l*. the average amount of Revenue paid into the Exchequer, 62,763,746*l*. and of Loans, 12,673,548*l*. making together 75,437,294*l*. and the average amount of the Total Expenditure of *Great Britain*, 82,205,066*l*. and that the average amount of Bank Netes, above 5*l*. was about 14,265,850*l*. and of Notes under 5*l*. about 5,283,330*l*. and that the amount of Gold Coin in circulation was greatly diminished.

15. *Resolved,* That it is the opinion of this Committee, That the situation of this Kingdom, in respect of its political and commercial relations with foreign Countries, as above stated, is sufficient, without any change in the internal value of its Currency, to account for the unfavourable state of the foreign Exchanges, and for the high price of Bullion.

16. *Resolved,* That it is the opinion of this Committee, That it is highly important that the Restriction on the payments in Cash of the Bank of *England* should be removed, whenever the political and commercial relations of the Country shall render it compatible with the public interest.

17. *Resolved,* That it is the opinion of this Committee, That, under the circumstances affecting the political and commercial relations of this Kingdom with foreign Countries, it would be highly inexpedient and dangerous now to fix a definite period for the removal of the Restriction of Cash payments at the Bank of *England,* prior to the term already fixed by the Act 44 *Geo.* III. c. 1. of six months after the conclusion of a Definitive Treaty of Peace.

————

These Resolutions were passed in the Committee on the same night, by a Majority of 82 to 42, and reported to the House on the following day, when the two first Resolutions were agreed to without a division ; and on the 15th, the Third Resolution was agreed to, by a Majority of 66 to 22, and the remaining Resolutions without a Division.

LIST OF PUBLICATIONS

In consequence of

THE REPORT OF THE COMMITTEE

OF THE

HOUSE OF COMMONS,

For inquiring into

𝕿𝖍𝖊 𝖍𝖎𝖌𝖍 𝕻𝖗𝖎𝖈𝖊 𝖔𝖋 𝕭𝖚𝖑𝖑𝖎𝖔𝖓,

In 1810—1811.

	£.	s.	d.
The Report on Bullion, together with Minutes of Evidence, and Account from the Select Committee, 8vo. Published in July, 1810, *Johnson*	0	12	0
Analysis of the Money Situation of Great Britain, 8vo. *Mackinlay*	0	1	6
Atkinson's (Jasper) Letter to a Member of Parliament, occasioned by the publication of the Report, 1810. *Hatchard*	0	3	6
Atkinson's (Jasper) Considerations, &c. written in 1802, *Hatchard*	0	3	6
A Review of the Controversy . *Budd*	0	3	0
Anonymous Letter on Paper Currency	0	1	6
Blake on Exchange, 8vo. *Lloyd*	0	3	0
Bosanquet's (Charles) Practical Observations on the Report of the Bullion Committee, Second Edition, with a Supplement, 1810, *J. M. Richardson*	0	5	0
Boase's (Mr.) Remarks on the New Doctrine, concerning the supposed Depreciation, 1811, *Nicol*	0	4	0

£. s. d.

£. s. d.

Huskisson's (W.) Question concerning the Depreciation of our Currency, 1810,   *Murray*   0 5 0

Hill's (John) Inquiry into the Causes of the High Price of Bullion   *Longman & Co.*   0 5 0

Hopkins's (T.) Bank Notes the Cause of the Disappearance of Guineas   *Murray*   0 4 0

Hoare's (P. R.) Examination of Sir John Sinclair's Observations   *Cadell & Davies*   0 4 0

Inquiry into the Relation of the Northern Powers, and Hints on Currency   *Hatchard*   0 3 6

Jackson's (R.) Speech   *Butterworth*   0 2 0

King on Bank Restriction, 8vo   *Cadell*   0 3 6

Koster's (Theodore) Short Statement of the Trade in Gold Bullion, Second Edition, enlarged   *Cadell & Davies*   0 3 6

Koster's (Theodore) further Observations, *Cadell & Davies*   0 2 0

Lyne's (Charles) Letter to the Rt. Hon. George Rose   *Richardson*   0 2 0

Letter to W. Huskisson on his late Publication, by a Proprietor of Bank Stock   0 2 0

Letter to Theodore Koster, Esq. *Cradock & Joy*   0 2 6

Letter on Paper Currency   0 2 6

Marryatt's (Joseph) Thoughts on the Expediency of Establishing a new Chartered Bank, *Hatchard*   0 3 0

Mushet's (Robert) Inquiry into the Effects produced in the National Currency, and the Rates of Exchange by the Bank Restriction Bill   *Baldwin*   0 0 0

Preface of Mr. Huskisson's Pamphlet examined   *Richardson*   0 1 0

Prentice's (David) Thoughts on the Repeal of the Bank Restriction Law   *Murray*   0 4 0

Pennyless's (Peter) Plain Inquiry into the Natural Value and Operation of Coin and Paper Money   *Whitmore & Fenn*   0 0 0

Phocion's Opinion   *Crosby*   0 1 0

Real Cause of the Depreciation explained   0 2 0

Ricardo on High Price of Bullion, 8vo, First Edit. 2s. 6d.   *Murray*   0 4 0

Ricardo's Appendix to his Fourth Edition of "The high Price of Bullion"   *Murray*   0 2 0

FINIS